# Tulasi Devi

# The Goddess of Devotion

Mata Amritanandamayi Center
San Ramon, California, United States

*Tulasi Devi,* the Goddess of Devotion
By Sarvaga and Gunavati

Published by
   Mata Amritanandamayi Center
   P.O. Box 613
   San Ramon, CA 94583
   United States

© 2015 by Mata Amritanandamayi Center, San Ramon, California, USA

All rights reserved. No part of this publication may be stored in a retrieval system, transmitted, reproduced, transcribed or translated into any language, in any form, by any means without the prior agreement and written permission of the publisher.

First edition by MA Center: 2015

In India:
   www.amritapuri.org

In USA:
   www.amma.org

In Europe:
   www.amma-europe.org

*We offer this book to our beloved Amma, the source of our inspiration, whose blessing has made this possible. We offer this book to Tulasi Devi, and seek Her forgiveness for any mistakes we may have made in describing Her glory. May this book be a humble offering for the benefit of all creation. May the Divine Mother guide us in awakening harmony on earth. By Her Grace, may this book bring healing and inspire Love for all beings and for Mother Nature.*

# Table of Contents

| | |
|---|---:|
| Sri Mata Amritanandamayi | 7 |
| The Incomparable One | 11 |
| **1. Ayurveda and the Healing Gifts of Tulasi** | **15** |
|     What is Ayurveda? | 15 |
|     Ayurveda and Medicinal Herbs | 18 |
| **2. Medical Research and Applications** | **24** |
|     Active Constituents | 25 |
|     Mode of Action | 26 |
|     Potential Medical Applications | 47 |
|     Precautions and Interactions | 51 |
| **3. Treatment Methods and Traditional Remedies** | **52** |
|     Tulasi Tea | 52 |
|     Tulasi Tincture | 54 |
|     Tulasi Essential Oil | 55 |
|     Tulasi Flower Essence | 58 |
|     Traditional Remedies: Tulasi Water, Juice, Powder and Paste | 60 |
| **4. Botany** | **63** |
|     Description | 64 |
|     Constituents | 66 |

Common Names of Tulasi in Various
Languages 66

## 5. Growing Tulasi Throughout the World 69
GreenFriends Distribution of Tulasi 69
How to Grow Tulasi 73
The Inner Tulasi ~ Developing Devotion
Within 109

## 6. Cultivation at Amma's Ashram in India 111
Amma's Tulasi Garden 111
The Divine Mother's Field 115

## 7. Insights and Experiences 123
The Wealth of Selflessness 123
The Living Goddess 125

## 8. Legends of Tulasi Devi 129
Praise from the Scriptures 139
Amma's Story of the Tulasi and Lotus 141

## 9. Traditional Worship and Rituals 146
Tulasi Puja 153
The Eight Sacred Names of Tulasi Devi
159
The 108 Names of Tulasi 159

## 10. Seeds of Hope 171
Hymn to Tulasi 173

## 11. References

Contributors to this book also include: Dr. Libby Maulder, Dr. Nibodhi Haas, Piyush, Lola, Greg, Advait, Prashanta, Janani, Vivek, Ambujam, Ramya, Jagannath, Pasupati and Kripa Prana.

# Preface

# Sri Mata Amritanandamayi

*"There is a rhythm to everything in the cosmos. The wind, the rain, the waves, the flow of our breath and heartbeat – everything has a rhythm. Similarly, there is a rhythm in life. Our thoughts and actions create the rhythm and melodies of our lives. When the rhythm of our thoughts is lost, it reflects in our actions. This will, in turn, throw off the very rhythm of life. Today, this is what we are seeing all around us.*

*"Today, the air is becoming more and more polluted; the water as well. Rivers are drying up. Forests are being destroyed. New diseases are spreading. If this continues, a huge disaster is in store for all of Nature and humanity."*
– *Amma*

Now, more than ever, it is evident that humanity must change in order to survive. The transformations that each of us makes in our own lives are vital for maintaining harmony on earth. We are blessed to be offered seeds of hope that inspire and guide us. This hope and inspiration is the very message of Amma's life.

Through Her extraordinary acts of love and self-sacrifice, Mata Amritanandamayi, or Amma (Mother), as She is more commonly known, has endeared Herself to millions of people around the world. Tenderly caressing everyone who comes to Her, holding them close to Her heart in a loving embrace, Amma shares boundless love with all, regardless of their beliefs, who they are, or why they have come to Her. In this simple yet powerful way, Amma is transforming the lives of countless people, helping their hearts to blossom, one embrace at a time. In the past 37 years, Amma has physically hugged more than 27 million people from around the world.

Amma's teachings are universal. Whenever Amma is asked about Her religion, She replies that Her religion is love. She does not ask anyone to believe in God or to change their faith, but only to inquire into their own real nature, and to believe in themselves.

Her tireless spirit of dedication to uplifting others has inspired a vast network of charitable activities, through which people are discovering the sense of peace that comes from selflessly serving others.

Amongst the wide array of charitable projects inspired by Amma are free homes for the poor, disaster relief, an orphanage, free food, medicine and pensions for destitute women, sponsored weddings for the poor, free legal aid, farmer suicide prevention, prisoner welfare programmes, hospitals and medical camps which offer free healthcare to the poor and many schools, colleges and educational programmes.

One branch of the tree of Amma's vast charitable projects is GreenFriends. This initiative began as a movement to inspire harmony and unity between Mother Nature and humanity. Since its inception in India in 2001, it has spread around the world, encouraging people to work for the preservation and protection of our environment.

Amongst its many activities, GreenFriends in India organises the planting of more than 100,000 trees a year, protects ancient sacred groves, re-educates the public on sustainable environmental practices, initiates and supports organic agricultural projects (especially in tribal areas) and conducts environmental awareness campaigns in schools. International GreenFriends activities include permaculture and alternative building workshops, tree-planting and restoration projects, nature meditation retreats, beekeeping, community organic gardens to provide produce for the homeless, environmental educational programmes for children, and projects to restore habitats and bio-diversity.

As a central aspect of GreenFriends, Amma has encouraged the reawakening of the ancient traditions that respect and worship Mother Nature. In this light, the traditional care and worship of Tulasi has been an integral part of the GreenFriends initiative. Amma emphasises that cultivating love for Tulasi can nurture awareness of the Divine within all things and can help to rekindle humanity's lost harmony with Mother Nature. She recommends this healing plant to many people who are sick with diseases ranging from colds to cancer, and has requested that it be grown by people throughout the world.

*Introduction*

# The Incomparable One

Tulasi means 'The Incomparable One'. She has been worshipped for thousands of years as an embodiment of the Divine Mother on earth. In legends, scriptures, medicinal practices, households, temples and hearts, Tulasi has grown and flourished as an undying symbol of the reverence for Nature inherent in the ancient culture of India.

The Divine Mother, exemplifying self-sacrifice and humility, has manifested Herself in this simple plant. Out of Her infinite compassion, She offers Her entire being for worship and medicine through the leaves, flowers, seeds and stems of the Tulasi plant. Her body, in the form of wood, is given to become beads on which the names of God are chanted. She teaches that even the simplest-looking plant is an embodiment of Divinity. Through this, we learn to behold God in even the smallest things and to honour the Divine in every aspect of creation.

Tulasi has the ability to heal countless diseases of the body, mind and spirit. As an embodiment of purity, She purifies the atmosphere around us, as well as our bodies, minds and souls. She is able to heal the physical eyes, and inwardly helps us to behold the vision of the Divine within all of creation. In the ancient scriptures of India (*Vedas*), Tulasi is praised as the purifier of sin. She is also renowned for cleansing internal and external poisons. She opens us to love and simultaneously our physical hearts are protected and strengthened.

Due to Tulasi's ability to treat countless diseases, it has long been a pillar of ayurvedic practice. Its holistic healing ability has led it to become an essential ingredient in cherished household remedies. Now, scientific explorations are confirming and popularising the properties of Tulasi that have been known and utilised since ancient times.

Tulasi reawakens the inherent longing in humanity to honour the divinity of Mother Nature. Now, more than ever, traditional practices that allow us to express our love for Nature and our gratitude for Her gifts, are needed in daily life. These practices create the awareness that is necessary for building a sustainable society. Perhaps, even more important is the mental harmony we

## Introduction – The Incomparable One

cultivate through worshipping Nature, which will be reflected in our environment. The simple ritual of worshipping the Tulasi plant, practised in the majority of Indian households for centuries, has become an inspiring symbol of expressing love and reverence for all of Creation.

Amongst its countless medicinal qualities, Tulasi is considered an adaptogenic herb, because it supports the body's capacity to deal with stress. As modern day stresses affect all of our lives, knowledge of this herb is essential for those who seek healing from the medicines that Nature offers.

People of different faiths, nationalities and backgrounds have found a common attraction to Tulasi. Even Tulasi's Latin name, *Ocimum sanctum,* communicates the recognition of Her sanctity. The desire to cultivate Tulasi in different countries and varying climates around the world has called for a communal wealth of experience in discovering how Tulasi should best be grown. The simple act of caring for this tender plant is an enriching experience that helps to awaken the motherhood within.

*"Anyone – woman or man – who has the courage to overcome the limitations of the mind can*

## *Tulasi Devi*, the Goddess of Devotion

*attain the state of universal motherhood. The love of awakened motherhood is a love and compassion felt not only towards one's own children, but towards all people, animals and plants, rocks and rivers – a love extended to all of nature, all beings. Indeed, to a woman in whom the state of true motherhood has awakened, all creatures are her children. This love, this motherhood, is Divine Love – and that is God."*     *– Amma*

From the wealth of Indian culture, we get a glimpse of the variety of traditional forms of worship and legends associated with the incarnation of the Goddess as Tulasi Devi. These rituals can be personally adapted into daily life, allowing us to experience the grace of a tangible connection with Tulasi and with the Divine.

Amma has encouraged the awareness of Tulasi to expand and spread around the world for the benefit of all creation. Tulasi's various methods of application and remedies are offered here to increase understanding of how to use this herb for personal healing. May the knowledge we cultivate help us on our journey to reconnect with own heart and with the heart of Mother Nature.

## Chapter 1

# Ayurveda and the Healing Gifts of Tulasi

For thousands of years, the outstanding depth and range of Tulasi's medicinal benefits have been expounded in the teachings of ayurveda. Modern scientific research is now confirming and adding to the already extensive body of knowledge regarding Tulasi's astounding healing powers. Commonly extolled as the 'Elixir of Life', Tulasi is used in hundreds of different traditional formulas. These remedies treat innumerable disorders of the blood, liver, kidney, heart, lungs, throat and mouth. Tulasi also treats the digestive, metabolic, reproductive and nervous systems.

## What is Ayurveda?

Ayurveda is the ancient wisdom of living in tune with our Self and our environment. Today, ayurveda is at the forefront of body-mind-spirit health practices. It has spread far beyond its traditional base and has gained attention worldwide.

Ayurveda, with its understanding of life and consciousness, has much to offer individuals, communities and Mother Earth as a whole. In this current age, Nature's harmony is rapidly declining. The planet and humanity are in a state of great imbalance. Resources are quickly diminishing, while war and sickness are on the rise. Ayurveda offers a realistic and practical solution to many of these problems.

Ayurvedic knowledge was born from the wisdom of the ancient sages and healers (*rishis*) and *yogis* of India. First transmitted from the Creator to the *rishis*, it was then passed down from healer to healer as an oral tradition for untold generations, before being transcribed around 5,000 BC. The *Rig Veda* contains the first documented scientific record of ayurveda. One of its verses states: "The sun should be a giver of happiness, the sky should be a giver of happiness, all trees and plants should be givers of happiness. All these should give us peace of mind, and even that peace should give us peace."

Ayurvedic knowledge imparts spiritual insights for living balanced, healthy and peaceful lives, while seeking the goal of Self-Realisation. It explains the nature of the universe and how to bring ourselves into harmony with it. A central principle in ayurveda is that everything in the universe is interconnected and interdependent.

The word *ayurveda* is composed of two words, *ayu*, meaning 'life' and *veda* meaning 'knowledge' or 'science', and literally translates as 'science of life'. The process of *ayu* is considered as a combined state of body, senses, emotions, psyche/mind and soul. It refers to all stages of life, including birth, childhood and adulthood; as well as the process of dying and going beyond death. Thus, ayurveda has individualised applications for all stages in the journey of life.

Overall, ayurveda provides practical and simple guidance regarding food and lifestyle so that people can maintain health, and those with physical imbalances can improve their condition. It is a tried and true system that helps to sustain long life and well-being. By incorporating these principles into daily life, we can support a harmonious earth, healthy bodies and positive relationships.

Several aspects of ayurveda make it a unique system of healing. As it is based on a constitutional model, recommendations are personalised for individual conditions. According to ayurveda, there are three main energetic forces, or *tridoshas*, which influence Nature and human beings. Each individual has their own unique combination of these three forces. The *tridoshas* are composed of the five elements that are present throughout the universe: ether, air, fire, water and earth. All of creation is a dance or a play of these five elements. The word *dosha* means 'impurity' or 'imbalance'. The three *doshas* (*vata, pitta* and *kapha)* are are responsible for biological, psychological and physiological processes in the body, mind and consciousness. Excess and deficiency of the *doshas* can lead to sickness. When the *doshas* are in harmony, they sustain balance within us.

## Ayurveda and Medicinal Herbs

Two of ayurveda's many branches of healing methods are the practice of herbal medicine and natural body care. Ayurvedic medicinal formulas and body care products are traditionally prepared without the use of chemicals, pesticides and herbicides. Using natural products is particularly valuable in the modern age, where imbalance and sickness often arise due to an overload of chemicals and artificial ingredients.

Tulasi is one of the most admired and respected ayurvedic herbs and is renowned for its powerful healing abilities. Tulasi is used in many ayurvedic medicines, teas and body care products. Tulasi is commonly used to treat cough, colds, flu, fever, congestion, bronchitis, asthma, sinusitis, earaches, headaches, diabetes, indigestion, gastric disorders, ulcers, high blood pressure, high cholesterol, sore throat, kidney stones, joint pain, rheumatoid arthritis, nausea, vomiting, cramping, mouth diseases, allergies, skin diseases, internal parasites, insect bites, numerous skin and eye disorders, malaria and cancer.

Although Tulasi is related to basil, it has a much stronger medicinal value than culinary basil. Perhaps no other plant on earth has been known to have such a vast range of medicinal and spiritual properties.

In ayurveda, herbs are classified according to their different natures as pure (*sattvic*), active (*rajasic*) or dull (*tamasic*). These three attributes are principles also used to describe various states of consciousness. Tulasi has the nature of pure consciousness *(sattva)*. *Sattvic* properties include pure light, righteous action, creativity and the power of observation. *Sattva* gives the power of discrimination, knowledge and the ability to know truth. The highest state of *sattva* manifests as peace, harmony, contentment, compassion, unconditional love, selflessness, devotion and faith. *Sattva* is also the state of equilibrium. When *sattva* prevails, there is peace and tranquillity.

Ayurveda looks at both diagnosis and treatment in the context of the *doshas*. The *vata dosha* consists of the ether and air elements; *pitta*, of fire; and *kapha*, of water and earth. The *doshas* govern all biological, physiological, and pathological changes in the body. *Vata*, *pitta* and *kapha* are present in various combinations in every cell, tissue and organ.

*Vata* regulates movement and governs the nervous system. *Kapha* is the principle of cohesion and functions through the body fluids. *Pitta* is the principle of bio-transformation and governs the metabolic processes in the body. In each individual, the three *doshas* manifest in different degrees, determining the physiological constitution (*prakriti*) of an individual. *Vata*, *pitta* and *kapha* are expressed differently in each human being according to the predominance of their different qualities (*gunas*).

In terms of the *doshas*, Tulasi calms *vata* and *kapha* while increasing *pitta*. An example of this is how Tulasi reduces anxiety and stress (*vata* qualities), decreases mucous (*kapha* substance) and promotes healthy digestion (*pitta* function).

Tulasi is a diaphoretic, meaning that it stimulates perspiration and circulation, and assists in eliminating toxins through the skin. It is also antispasmodic, antibacterial and antiseptic and supports the plasma, blood, marrow, nerves and reproductive tissues.

Taking Tulasi removes excess *vata* from the colon, and therefore increases nutrient absorption while strengthening and rejuvenating the nervous system. As a tonic for the nervous system, it promotes mental clarity and a heightened sense of awareness. Tulasi is a powerful and unique medicine for stress and stress-related diseases. As it calms the mind, Tulasi can assist in deepening one's meditation practice.

Tulasi removes mucus caused by excess *kapha* in the lungs, respiratory tract and nasal passages, thereby increasing vital life force (*prana*) and circulation. The increase in *prana* helps to ward off asthma, bronchitis, rhinitis, allergies and other respiratory symptoms. Tulasi's beneficial effect on the respiratory system leads to increased lung capacity and cell respiration.

## *Tulasi Devi,* the Goddess of Devotion

Tulasi works specifically to counter coughs, colds, sinus congestion, headaches, arthritis, rheumatism, fevers and abdominal distension. Because if its ability to purify the lymphatic system and induce perspiration, Tulasi has the unique power to combat fevers, no matter what the cause.

Tulasi promotes good digestion by igniting digestive fire (*agni*), and is also useful in reducing excess weight, while regulating the spleen and pancreas. This, in turn, lowers and balances blood sugar and cholesterol.

In ayurveda, the specific properties of herbs are always taken into account. It is essential to know the details of herbal properties so that they can be applied properly for treatment. *Virya* is the energy/power or potency of the herb. *Virya* is an important factor in determining herbal usage. It is determined as either heating or cooling for the body.

The post-digestive effect that the herb has on the body is called *vipaka*. This effect correlates to the process of absorption and elimination. The six tastes (*rasa*) are: sweet, sour, salty, bitter, pungent and astringent. Each of the tastes is composed of two of the five elements. Sweet is made up of water and earth. Bitter and astringent are both air and ether. Salty is water and fire. Sour is earth and fire. Pungent is fire and air.

The qualities of the herbs are known as *gunas*. They are grouped into ten complimentary pairs, such as hot and cold, dry and wet, etc. Knowledge of the *guna* further helps in determining the treatment according to an individual's constitution.

## Ayurvedic Properties of Tulasi:

***Rasa*** (taste) – pungent (*katu*) & bitter (*tikta*)
***Guna*** (quality) – light *(laghu)* & dry (*ruksha*)
***Virya*** (potency) – hot (*ushna*)
***Vipaka*** (taste after digestion) – pungent (*katu*)

Although Tulasi addresses a variety of chronic and acute illnesses, it can also be taken as a preventative herb to boost immunity and assist the body's natural process of maintaining health. Continued use makes one less susceptible to common illnesses and increases energy levels.

# Chapter 2

# Medical Research and Applications

*"Tulasi leaves are highly medicinal. The leaves won't decay, even if plucked and kept for several days; the medicinal potency remains. The medicinal value of Tulasi leaves, which was known to the ancient rishis eons ago, has now been proven by modern scientific experiments."*
*– Amma*

Medical research is just beginning to unlock some of the miraculous healing properties of Tulasi (*Ocimum sanctum*). So far, research has been limited, because it has been conducted primarily in vitro (in test tubes) or on animals, rather than people. The studies aim to identify the main active constituents, their likely mode of action and the medical conditions that may benefit from Tulasi. The results are impressive, and, in most instances, support the traditional uses. As a result of this research and the increasing awareness of the value of traditional herbal medicine, interest in Tulasi is dramatically increasing. Additional comprehensive research is needed to fully understand and scientifically verify the healing potential of this sacred plant.

Outlined below are the active constituents of *Ocimum sanctum* that have been scientifically identified to date. Their mode of action and possible clinical applications with supporting medical research is provided.

## Active Constituents

*Ocimum sanctum* (*OS*) contains alkaloids, fats, carbohydrates, proteins, glycosides, phenols, saponins, tannins, terpenes, flavonoids, vitamins and minerals. Its essential oil has been shown to contain more than 57 compounds, the level of which varies depending on where it is grown and when it is harvested (1).

The oil mainly contains volatile terpenes and phenols including eugenol (a major pharmacological component), methyl eugenol, methyl ether, caryophyllene, terpine-4-ol, decylaldehyde, salinene, alpha and beta-pinene, camphene, carvacol, terpene-urosolic acid, urosolic acid, oleanic acid, juvocimene1 and 2, thymol, rhymol, camphor, xanthomicrol, caffeate, myrcenol and nerol.

The fixed oil of the seeds also contains stearic, palmitic, oleic, linoleic and linolenic acids (2). The leaves contain vitamin A, vitamin C, calcium, iron, zinc, manganese, selenium, chlorophyll and sodium (3 p. 53).

## Mode of Action

### Adaptogenic

*OS* is a powerful adaptogen; meaning that it increases the body's non-specific resistance to stress, allowing one to more easily adapt to adverse physical, chemical or biologically-stressful circumstances. Adaptogenic herbs like *OS* often have a wide range of properties such as being antioxidant, anti-carcinogenic, immuno-modulatory, hypo-cholesterolaemic, hypoglycaemic, hepato-protective, chemopreventative, and anti-inflammatory. Other relevant properties that increase stamina include an anabolic effect, increased muscle strength, and increased utilisation of oxygen. An animal study showed that *OS* achieved a superior level of physical performance, endurance and physical stamina than certain modern synthetic drugs and Siberian or Korean ginseng, two of the most commonly-used adaptogens. In addition, it produced fewer side effects and had a calming action, as opposed to the stimulating action of ginseng. The combination of its calming and adaptogenic effects is ideal in the modern world, where stress is invariably a factor in debility and ill-health (3 p. 32).

## Anabolic

Enhanced protein synthesis with increased muscle mass and strength was observed following the ingestion of *OS* in animal studies. This may be beneficial in states of debility, such as old age and cancer (4).

## Analgesic

Several animal studies have shown *OS* to have an analgesic effect (5)(60). In one study, the alcoholic leaf extract of *OS* was found to have analgesic activity. It was suggested that the analgesic action of *OS* is exerted both centrally as well as peripherally, and involves an inter-play between various neurotransmitter systems (60).

## Anti-allergy

There are four main types of allergies. The most common is called Type 1 Hypersensitivity, which occurs in asthma, hay fever, allergic skin rashes and food allergies. This involves production of IGE antibodies in response to an allergen. These antibodies then bind to mast cells and trigger the release of histamine and other substances. This causes the symptoms of allergies such as inflammation, itch, and constriction of airways. In this situation, elevated levels of IGE antibodies, eosinophils and histamine are commonly found. Type 4 or Delayed Hypersensitivity occurs when an allergen contacts the skin of an allergy sufferer, and after one to two days, an area of local skin inflammation is produced at the contact site. This is a T cell-mediated reaction.

Tulasi's anti-allergy effect has been observed in the treatment of asthma. It produces a reduction in bronchospasm, mortality and eosinophil count in the blood and sputum of asthma suffers (9). It has also been effective in Tropical Pulmonary Eosinophillia, an allergic condition with a very high eosinophil count, which is associated with bronchospasms or wheezing (10).

Studies have also shown that *OS* exerts direct effect on mast cells, stabilising them so that less histamine is released. In animal studies, the effect of ursolic acid, a triterpene from *OS* leaves, was found to exhibit a significant protective effect on the mast cell membrane. This occurs by prevention, de-granulation and decrease in the quantity of histamine released by an allergenic compound (11). Another study involving animals showed that the ethanolic extract (50%) of fresh leaves of *OS*, its volatile oil (from fresh leaves) and fixed oil (from the seeds) had anti-asthmatic activity and anti-inflammatory activity, inhibiting the carrageenan, serotonin, histamine and PGE-2-induced inflammation, following topical application (12).

Studies have also shown that *OS* decreases the allergic response mediated by T cell hypersensitivity. A group of people given *OS* for four weeks before an allergen was applied to the skin, had a more marked protective response with a reduction in inflammation. This was due to an increase in cell-mediated immunity (13)(14)(15).

## Anti-asthma

*OS* has been shown to have an anti-asthmatic effect by reducing the frequency and severity of asthma attacks and the associated death rate. Additionally, it increases the lung function in asthma sufferers (16). The mechanism of this is probably complex, involving anti-allergy, anti-inflammatory, antioxidant and anxiolytic effects. (See anti-allergy section above for further details). Components of OS (myrcenol and nerol) have also been demonstrated to have anti-asthma activity (17).

## Antibacterial

Many in vivo and in vitro studies have shown that the essential oil of OS has antibacterial activity against staphylococci and other bacteria (35)(3 p.39). Studies also showed some anti tubercular activity (3 p.39). The leaves and essential oil demonstrate this property and may be used topically on abscesses and other localised infections. Fresh OS leaf extract was effective in the treatment of gram-negative oral infections and inhibiting against human plaque cultures (36). An in vitro study, conducted in 2005, showed Neisseria gonorrhoea clinical isolates and WHO strains were sensitive to extracts of *Ocimum sanctum* (37).

A further study found that aqueous and alcoholic extracts of OS (60mg) inhibited enteric pathogens and Candida albicans in the laboratory. Aqueous extract showed wider zones of inhibition, when compared to alcoholic extract. It also showed wider zones of inhibition for Klebisella, E. coli, Proteus and Staphylococcus aureus. Alcoholic extract showed wider zones for vibrio cholera (38).

### Anti-cancer

The anti-cancer effect of OS has been demonstrated in many animal studies using different parts of the plant. OS demonstrated the ability to prevent cancers and slow the progression of already-established cancers, as well as increasing longevity (68)(69). Its potent antioxidant, anti-inflammatory and immuno-modulating properties are most likely responsible for these effects.

In one animal study, the seed oil reduced the carcinogenic effect of a known carcinogenic chemical. The study suggested that the chemo-preventive activity of the oil is partly attributable to its antioxidant properties (68). Another animal study showed treatment with the leaf extract of OS significantly elevated the activities of cytochrome p-450, cytochrome b5, aryl hydrocarbon hydroxylase, glutathione S-transferase and glutathione, all of which are important in the detoxification of carcinogens as well as mutagens (31). Extracts of *OS* have been shown to protect against chemically-induced oral cancer in animals. This effect was most marked with the aqueous extract (70). In another animal study, administration of aqueous and ethanolic extracts of *OS* mediated a significant reduction in tumour volume and an increase in life span (69). Ursolic acid, found in *OS,* demonstrated remarkable inhibitory activity against tumour promotion (71). Ursolic acid and oleanolic acid have been recommended for skin cancer therapy in Japan for humans following clinical trials which showed impressive inhibition of skin cancer in animals studies (66).

## Anticoagulant

One study showed that *OS* fixed oil increased blood-clotting time. The percentage increase was comparable to aspirin and could be due to inhibition of platelet aggregation (78).

## Anti-depressant

OS has been observed to have anti-depressant effects in clinical practice. This may be due to the direct increase in levels of serotonin neurotransmitters in the brain, such as an increase in levels of serotonin (3 p. 30). One study showed that OS extract had an effect comparable to that of disipramine, an anti-depressant drug (63).

## Anti-fertility

A variety of different studies have suggested that *OS* has abortifacient and anti-fertility properties in women (59). In animal studies, extracts of *OS* decreased female fertility by 60 and 80%, respectively (83)(84). In males, study results showed decreased sperm production, motility and forward velocity (85)(86). Ursolic acid has anti-oestrogen properties, and is the constituent of *OS* thought to be responsible for the anti-fertility effect (82)(86).

## Anti-fungal

OS has been shown to have strong anti-fungal properties present in the essential oil (3 p. 42).

## Anti-inflammatory

Leaf extracts of *OS* inhibit both acute and chronic inflammation, and also have analgesic and antipyretic effects (5). The fixed oil in the seeds of *OS* was also found to have significant anti-inflammatory activity. This is likely due to the presence of linolenic acid and other phytonutrients, e.g., ursolic acid, present in the oil, which significantly inhibits cyclo-oxygenase-2 (Cox-2) (6). Several studies have found *OS* to be effective for arthritis (7)(8).

## Antioxidant

A healthy body has a balance between reductive and oxidative mechanisms. Oxidative stress occurs in the body when there is a large rise in reactive oxygen substances, including free radicals and peroxides. These substances can damage all cellular components, including proteins, lipids and DNA, causing diseases such as atherosclerosis, dementia, Parkinson's disease, cancer, ageing, cataract formation, macular degeneration and auto-immune disease. An increase in oxidative substances can be caused by exposure to chemicals (e.g. insecticides, pesticides, toxic chemicals and drugs, trans-fatty acids, smoke, pollution), trauma, irradiation, UV radiation, electromagnetic radiation, temperature extremes, infections and stress.

Oxidative stress is prevented in a healthy body by a large number of antioxidant enzymes, which can detoxify reactive substances and repair cellular damage. These include superoxides dismutase (SOD), catalase, glutathione peroxidase, sulfiredoxin, glutathione-S-transferases, aldehydes and dehydrogenase. Antioxidants in our diet can help maintain this balance. *OS* is a powerful antioxidant containing multiple compounds with this action, including eugenol, rosmarinic acid, apigenin, urosolic acid, cirsilineol, cirsimaritin, isothymusin, isothymonin, vitamin C, vitamin A and selenium (18). Of these, eugenol is thought to be the most powerful antioxidant.

The antioxidant effect of *OS* seed oil was observed in an animal study in 2006. Decreased lipid peroxidation and increased reduced-glutathione content in the blood were observed after ingestion of *OS* seed oil (19). Another study reported that *OS* has significant ability to scavenge highly-reactive free radicals. *OS* was found to protect against free-radical liver damage in humans and other animals after exposure to carbon tetrachloride, a highly hepatoxic chemical (20)(21)(22)(23). Other studies (24) confirmed that *OS* gave protection against free-radical damage to the liver. In 1992, they showed that the cardiac lipid membranes were protected in a similar way by *OS*. Shade-dried leaf powder of the plant was extracted with water and alcohol, and then fractionated with different solvents. Both extracts and their fractions had in vitro, anti-lipid peroxidative activity at very low concentrations. In vivo, erythrocyte lipid-peroxidation was inhibited. The extract also provided significant liver and aortic tissue protection from peroxidative damage (25).

Regular oral administration of *OS* in an animal study was found to augment cardiac endogenous antioxidants, and thereby prevent chemical-induced myocardial necrosis (26). Another animal study showed *OS* had a protective effect by increasing antioxidant levels in the heart and reducing myocardial muscle oedema (27). Animal studies done in 1996 and 1998, showed *OS* afforded, in vivo, protection against radiation-induced cytogenetic damage. Free radical scavenging was thought to be the likely mechanism of the *OS* protection (28) (29). In 2004, an animal study established antioxidant and neuro-protective effects of *OS* on transient and long-term hypo-perfusion of the brain (30).

Further studies suggest that the cancer-protective effect observed with *OS* may be partially due to its antioxidant properties (31)(32). In 1998, Pandaand Kar showed that extracts from *OS* decreased markers of oxidative stress and increased levels of antioxidant enzymes, superoxides dismutase and catalase. *OS* leaf is known to have prophylactic action and the ability to inhibit the progress of cataract formation. Oxidative damage by free radicals is believed to be the major cause of cataracts; thus, the anti-cataract ability of *OS* is closely linked with its antioxidant activity (33) (34).

## Anti-parasitic and Anti-protozoal

The essential oil of *OS* and eugenol, tested in vitro, showed potent anti-parasitic and anti-worm activity (43). An *OS* leaf extract was found to be inhibitory to Serata digitata, a variety of filarial worm in cattle (44). It has been demonstrated that *OS* has a direct effect in prevention and treatment of malaria (45).

## Antipyretic

OS has been clinically proven to reduce fever (5).

## Anti-stress

*OS* has been shown to have a powerful anti-stress effect (61). This has been extensively researched by Dr. Narendra Singh's team (3). He found this was achieved through a variety of methods including; a direct effect on the adrenal glands and cortisone synthesis, altering levels of neurotransmitters in the brain (increasing adrenaline, noradrenaline, dopamine and decreasing serotonin) and increasing production of the enzyme succinate dehydrogenase in the brain, which is important for energy generation in times of stress. He also found that *OS* had a calming effect, reducing aggressive behaviour in animals. *OS* increased the body's ability to use oxygen, which may increase endurance and the ability to cope with stress.

Results of another study suggest that the anti-stress activity of *OS* is partly attributable to its antioxidant properties (62). Further studies verify *OS* anti-stress effects. One study suggests a central nervous system stimulant and/or anti-stress activity from methanol extract, obtained from the roots of *OS* (63). Studies have shown that extracts of *OS* leaves were effective in alleviating stress-induced changes in animals (64)(65)(27). Additionally, *OS* showed a mild tranquillising effect in animals.

**Anti-thyroidism**

In 1998, an animal study found *OS* leaf extract decreased levels of T4 but did not alter levels of T3 or T3/T4 (81). This may have some relevance for overactivity of the thyroid gland.

## Anti-tussive

Anti-tussive refers to the ability to reduce cough. Aqueous and methanolic extracts of *OS* exhibited anti-tussive effect by central action, and appeared to mediate both the opioid system and GABA-ergic system (37).

## Anti-ulcer

The fixed seed oil of *OS* has been found to have powerful anti-ulcer and anti-inflammatory activity, reducing the occurrence of gastric ulcers (55). Multiple studies have shown *OS* prevents peptic ulceration in animals that are exposed to chemical or physical stresses that normally induce ulceration (3 p.30).

A study in 2005 demonstrated *OS* to have both ulcer prevention and healing properties by significantly inhibiting the acid-pepsin secretion and lipid peroxidation, its antioxidant effect. It also increased the gastric defensive factors like increased mucin secretion, and life span of mucosal cells. It did not induce mucosal cell proliferation. Other studies had similar findings (56)(57). A human clinical study showed that *OS* was useful in the prevention and treatment of stress-related gastric ulcers (58). Bactericidal properties may help eradicate Helicobacter pylori, the bacteria now known to be the major cause of peptic ulceration.

## Anti-viral

Studies have shown the effectiveness of *OS* juice and powdered leaves against viral infections in plants and chickens, respectively (3 p. 39)(39). It has been used effectively to treat viral hepatitis and Japanese Viral Encephalitis Type B in humans (40)(41). A water-soluble component of a close relative of *OS* was found to have some anti-HIV effects. It was shown to increase total T lymphocyte (white cell) count and inhibit HIV-1 reverse transcription (42). Research has shown that *OS* produces an enhanced response in cellular immunity, with increased white cell numbers, and a marked protective response. This is probably the main explanation for observed anti-viral activity of *OS*.

## Cardio-protective

Several animal studies have shown *OS* to be cardio-protective when the heart is subjected to certain stresses. In a study done in 2006, *OS* produced increased ventricular function, increased endogenous levels of antioxidants in the myocardium and suppression of oxidative stress (26). This increase in antioxidants was confirmed in another study (27). Other mechanisms may also be involved in its cardio-protective effect, such as stress reduction, general adaptogenic properties and its mild anticoagulant effect.

## Chemoprotective

The chemoprotective effect of *OS* has been demonstrated in multiple studies using a variety of noxious chemicals affecting different organs. *OS* significantly reduced the level of damage caused by mercury, carbon tetrachloride, antituberculous drugs, paracetamol (affecting the liver) and isoproterol (affecting the heart)(3 p.32, 33)(26). This was achieved through a variety of mechanisms including its powerful antioxidant effect.

## Enhanced Cognitive Processes

A study conducted in 2006 showed extracts of *OS* improved memory and learning abilities (67).

## Hypoglycaemic Action

Numerous studies have shown *OS*, both as an extract and as a dietary component, to have hypoglycaemic action in diabetes (47)(48)(49)(50). This effect may be due to both a reduction in insulin resistance and to an increase in insulin secretion (51)(52)(53). The results of a randomised, placebo-controlled, crossover trial on the effects of a leaf extract of *OS* on patients with Type 2 diabetes, showed that treatment causes a significant decrease in fasting and post-prandial blood glucose levels, with no adverse effects. In this study, reductions of 17.6% of fasting glucose levels and 7.3% of post-prandial blood glucose were observed. Total cholesterol levels also showed a mild reduction. The results from this study suggest that *OS* may be prescribed as an adjunct to dietary therapy and drug treatment for mild-to-moderate, non-insulin dependent diabetes (52).

In another study, 120 patients with Type 2 diabetes were given a composite combining *OS* leaves with four other Ayurvedic herbs, over a three-month period. The study showed impressive results. Application of the composite resulted in a reduction of fasting blood sugar, LDL ('bad') cholesterol and insulin resistance, and an increase in good cholesterol. The composite in this study was shown to cause a reduction of insulin resistance in the patients (54).

## Hypotensive

An animal study found *OS* fixed oil produced a hypotensive effect (lowering of blood pressure), which seems to be due to its peripheral vasodilatory action (78).

## Immuno-modulating

The human immune system involves a complex interplay of different organs and systems, different types of white blood cells, antibodies (also called immunoglobulins), hormones and active proteins involved in the Complement Cascade. Humoral immunity refers to immunity due to the production of antibodies from B Lymphocytes. Cell-mediated immunity refers to the immunity due to T lymphocytes (Suppresser T Cells, Helper T cells and Cytotoxic T cells) that directly kill cells infected with viruses.

*OS* is said to modulate the immune system since it strengthens or stimulates it when needed, as with infections and cancer. However, it reduces or down-regulates it when the immune system has become overactive, such as with allergies. In a study involving animals, *OS* seed oil was shown to modulate both humoral and cell-mediated immune responsiveness. It was postulated that these immuno-modulatory effects may be mediated by GABA-ergic pathways. The immunosuppressive effect of stress was blocked when the animals were treated with *OS* leaf oil (75). Other experiments in animals confirm that *OS* has the capability to increase antibody response and levels of white blood cells (neutrophils and lymphocytes) when the immune system is challenged (76) (39)(3 p. 35, 38).

An animal study investigating the response to tumour-inducing chemicals showed an alcoholic extract of *OS* decreased the numbers of tumours formed. There was an increased infiltration of polymorphonuclear, mononuclear and lymphocytic cells, decreased ornithine decarboxylase activity with concomitant enhancement of interleukin-1beta (IL-1beta) and tumour necrosis factor-alpha (TNF-alpha) in the serum. This implied the anti-proliferative and immunomodulatory activity of leaf extract in vivo (77).

## Insecticide and Insect Repellent Properties

*OS* has been shown to be an insecticide against mosquitoes, ticks and their larvae. *OS* has been called the 'mosquito plant', as it is proven to have mosquito repellent properties (3 p. 39). A more

## Medical Research and Applications

recent study found *OS* also has honeybee repellent properties (46).

**Liver Protective**

The hepato-protective effect of *OS* has been verified in many studies involving humans and animals, who were exposed to liver toxins (see Chemoprotective Mode of Action) (3 p. 32, 33). This mechanism is not fully understood, but probably involves the powerful antioxidant and anti-inflammatory properties of *OS*. Two further studies showed oleanolic acid and ursolic acid, compounds found in *OS*, are effective in protecting against chemically-induced liver injury. The mechanism of hepato-protection by these two compounds may involve the inhibition of toxicant activation and the enhancement of the body defence systems. Oleanolic acid has been used in China as an oral drug for human liver disorders (71)(80).

**Nutritive**

*OS* contains calcium, phosphorous, iron, zinc, vitamin A, vitamin C, selenium, manganese, chlorophyll and photo-nutrients (3 p. 53). *OS* supports the digestion, absorption and use of nutrients from food and herbs.

## Radioprotective

Several animal studies have shown *OS* leaf extract to be radioprotective, protecting normal living cells against the damaging effects of ionising radiation. This was due to its free radical scavenging and antioxidant activity (28)(72)(29)(73). One of these studies found that tumour cells were not protected from this damage mechanism, indicating that *OS* is not contraindicated during chemotherapy (72). The radioprotective effects of two flavonoids, orientin and vicenin, obtained from the leaves of *OS*, were studied in animals, and viewing the low dose needed for protection, were concluded to be promising for human radiation protection (74).

## Reduction in Cholesterol and Triglycerides Levels

Saponins in *OS* bind with cholesterol and some of its precursors to cause a mild reduction in cholesterol, LDL ('bad') cholesterol and triglycerides, and variable change in the level of protective HDL cholesterol. Both human and animal studies have confirmed this (3 p. 39).

**Smooth Muscle Relaxant**

This action has been found in the fresh leaves and flower tops. It reduces peristalsis and slows down the gut transit time. It is also relaxes bronchospasm in asthma (59).

**Vascular Effects**

*OS* reduces oxidative damage to vascular endothelium (25). This theoretically should produce a reduction in atherosclerotic plaque development. A study was conducted in 2006 in which diabetic animals were fed vitamin E and *OS* alone and in combination. After 16 weeks, a lowering in blood sugar levels and lipid levels took place. There was an improvement in diabetic retinopathy, both individually and when used in combination. With the combination, the retina returned to normal, which may be due to an antioxidant effect (79).

# Potential Medical Applications

With such an extraordinary array of different properties, *OS* has the potential to help many different medical conditions. It is no surprise that its name means 'The Incomparable One'. Few other herbal or pharmaceutical medicines have such a wide variety of clinical applications and modes of action. *OS* can generally be used safely and effectively alongside allopathic medicines to expedite recovery.

Below are listed some medical conditions that, on the basis of current research, may benefit from treatment with *OS*. More human clinical trials are needed to verify these recommendations.

### Cardiovascular System

*OS* can be used to treat hypertension (especially when associated with stress), dyslipidaemia (elevated cholesterol and triglycerides), atherosclerosis and ishaemic heart disease. *OS* generally supports impaired heart functioning, protects the heart (from stress, cardiotoxic drugs, chemicals and radiation.)

### Central Nervous System

*OS* can be used for stress, depression, impaired memory, impaired cognition, dementia, degenerative conditions including ageing, recovery after stroke, protection against lack of oxygen, noxious chemicals, drugs and radiation toxicity. It may also be used for headache and general pain relief.

**Endocrine System**

*OS* may treat diabetes, has an anti-ageing effects and increases stamina and well-being.

**Eyes**

*OS* offers a possible benefit for cataract formation, macular degeneration and conjunctivitis, and can treat diabetic retinopathy.

**Gastrointestinal System**

*OS* can treat oral and periodontal infections and improves appetite and digestion. It reduces indigestion and gastro-esophageal reflux, peptic ulcers, irritable bowel syndrome, nausea and vomiting, diarrhoea and intestinal infections. It can also be used in cases of infective hepatitis, to improve impaired liver function, to protect the liver from noxious chemicals and drugs and to reduce radiation damage.

**Immune System**

*OS* has been proven to help in cases of infections. Its antiviral properties make it effective in treating colds and influenza, hepatitis, Japanese encephalitis and HIV. It is also antibacterial, anti-fungal, anti- protozoan (malaria) and anti-parasitic (e.g. anti-filarial). It may be beneficial in treating cancer, auto-immune disorders and allergies including asthma.

## Musculoskeletal System

*OS* may be beneficial for all types of arthritis including osteoarthritis, rheumatoid and other inflammatory types. It can additionally be used in cases of general inflammation and muscular weakness, as it increases muscular mass and strength.

## Respiratory System

*OS* can be used for viral and bacterial infections (e.g. colds and flu), sinusitis, bronchitis, allergies (rhinitis, hay fever, asthma, pulmonary, pulmonary eosinophillia) and lung cancer. It can also be used to help protect the lungs from damage due to radiation, carcinogens and toxic substances in general.

## Skin

*OS* promotes wound healing, and is antiseptic and anti-infective (against bacterial and fungal infections). It is also beneficial for eczema and psoriasis, works as an insect repellent and plays a possible role in the prevention of skin cancers.

**General**

*OS* may assist during convalescence and with general debility, fever and chronic fatigue syndrome. It can offer nutritional support and protection against general stresses (e.g. trauma, temperature extremes, emotional imbalances, toxic chemicals, carcinogens, radiation, UV light, noise, physical stress and electromagnetic radiation).

## Precautions and Interactions

*OS* is considered a safe herb; and it is available without restriction throughout the world. There are no known contraindications, toxic side effects or documented herb/drug interactions. It may act synergistically with anticoagulants, hypoglycaemics, antidepressants and anti-stress medication. Theoretically, it may worsen hypoglycaemia; but this is not verified. Possibly avoid large doses if trying to conceive.

## Chapter 3

# Treatment Methods and Traditional Remedies

As Tulasi has an extensive range of medicinal benefits addressing various bodily systems, it is utilised in many diverse forms. These include tea, tincture, essential oil, flower essence, juice, powder and paste.

## Tulasi Tea

Most commonly, people receive the benefits of Tulasi by enjoying it as an aromatic, calming tea. Tulasi tea has a pleasant flavour, and a relaxing, yet deeply rejuvenating effect. This tea is an easy and effective method for receiving Tulasi's healing attributes.

Tulasi tea inhibits enzymes that contribute to inflammation and arthritic pain. It also enhances the adrenal function by lowering cortisol levels. This reduces the negative effects of stress. Tulasi tea is also excellent for digestive disorders, regulating blood pressure and building immunity.

## Treatment Methods and Traditional Remedies

Bring water to a boil and pour one cup over a teaspoon of fresh Tulasi leaves, one-half teaspoon of dry Tulasi leaves (or tea bag) or one-third teaspoon of powder. Cover and allow it to steep for at least 20 minutes. The longer it steeps, the more medicinal properties will be extracted from the leaves.

Tulasi tea can be enjoyed several times a day. It is a wonderful replacement for coffee and tea, because it offers a more balanced and sustained energy. Taken in the evening, it can melt away the tensions of the day, helping to bring deeper, more restful sleep. Children love it with honey, and parents appreciate its ability to calm hyperactivity.

Tulasi tea has been used for thousands of years to prevent and minimise the symptoms of colds and flu, support upper respiratory health, reduce fevers and promote overall health. When treating colds, flus and other more severe illnesses, it is suggested to increase the amount and strength of the tea. This can be taken three to six times daily, until health improves. This will help lessen the duration of the cold/flu. Drinking Tulasi tea with added honey and ginger can soothe sore throats.

## Tulasi Tincture

Tulasi tincture is made from placing a high concentration of plant material in a base of alcohol or glycerine. The alcohol/glycerine extracts the concentrated medicinal properties of the plant. Tincture is traditionally made in accordance with the cycles of the moon. It has long been recognised that the lunar energies increase the potency of medicinal herbs.

The process of making tincture condenses a high volume of therapeutic properties into a small quantity of medicine. As they use only a small amount of plant material, tinctures are also ecologically sustainable. For those who are unable to grow enough Tulasi to provide an ongoing source of tea, making a tincture can provide a sufficient supply of medicine.

While it works on the physical, mental, and spiritual levels of the body, it is especially powerful for treating physical ailments and stimulating the immune system. Tincture is absorbed more rapidly than other forms of internal medicine, as it passes straight through the mucous membrane into the bloodstream. It is often recommended for those with serious illnesses, such as cancer.

Tulasi tincture additionally help protect against mercury toxicity.

For people who are travelling, or those who do not have time for making tea, tincture is a convenient, condensed form of Tulasi. As the tincture is extremely concentrated, only a very small amount should be taken each day. Take two to three drops in a glass of water or place the drops directly under the tongue. Take this treatment two to three times a day. During acute sickness, it can be taken three to five times a day.

## Tulasi Essential Oil

Aromatherapy is one of the oldest forms of natural medicine. Aromatherapy uses the volatile oils of plants, which have been distilled or extracted into a highly concentrated form. For more than 6,000 years, essential oils have been used around the world to heal physical and psychological diseases. Essential oils are the condensed life force of the plant.

In the spirit of ecological conservation, it is important to understand the potency of essential oils. It takes very large quantities of plant material to make even one drop of essential oil. In this light, use essential oils in moderation and with care. As essential oils are one of the highest sources of antioxidants, they protect against free radical damage. They also assist in delivering nutrients in our bodies. Essential oils oxygenate tissues and cells. This is very valuable at a time when the planet is experiencing rising levels of air pollution, pesticides and chemicals, as these pollutants reduce the amount of oxygen in the human body.

To give some perspective on how potent essential oils are, one drop of essential oil gives the same benefit as 30 cups of herbal tea. Due to this strong potency, smelling and diffusing oils are highly-activated ways of introducing them into the body. When essential oils are inhaled, they pass through the blood/brain barrier directly to the limbic brain where emotions, memory, and regulatory functions are seated. This creates an immediate shift in the entire physical body and also brings deep transformation to the mind and spirit.

Essential oils can be used on the body, mixed into massage oil, dropped into bath water, burned in a diffuser, or simply smelled to provide therapeutic benefits. One especially effective method for rapid absorption is massaging oil along the spine or onto the feet.

## Treatment Methods and Traditional Remedies

Like other essential oils, Tulasi, when applied externally, will penetrate the pores, enter into the bloodstream and affect adjacent organs. From there, it will circulate rapidly to areas most in need of healing. Remember, when placing oils directly on the skin, it is recommended to use them sparingly or to dilute them in a carrier such as organic almond or jojoba oil. Tulasi essential oil is intended for external use only. Due to its high potency, if taken internally, it may aggravate the stomach lining.

Tulasi essential oil works on both physical and emotional aspects of health. It gives a giant boost to the immune system and helps heal disease, while opening the heart and cultivating devotion.

Therapeutic grade essential oil of Tulasi has antibacterial, antifungal and antiviral properties. Steam inhalation with Tulasi essential oil is especially good for clearing sinus congestion, headaches and infections. Simply smelling the oil directly can help with these conditions as well.

Tulasi essential oil can also be used as a preventive against insect stings or bites. For an insect repellent, mix a few drops of Tulasi essential oil with eucalyptus and/or citronella essential oils and apply to the body. For some, applying the essential oil directly on the body may be too strong. In this case, it can be diluted in water or with carrier oils. In case of insect stings or bites, Tulasi essential oil may also be applied to the affected area to reduce itching and to help prevent infection.

## Tulasi Flower Essence

Flower essences are water-based solutions, which contain the essential energies of flowers. They are made by floating flowers in purified water and allowing the light of the sun, moon and/or stars to help the water absorb the energy signature of each flower. The structure of the water molecule is extremely sensitive and can store these plant energies. The extracted essence is preserved with alcohol to make a mother essence. The mother essence is diluted with water and alcohol to create a stock bottle. This is further diluted to prepare the dose bottle. Just as in homeopathy, dilution actually makes the essence stronger.

Flower essence remedies have been used by native peoples of the world for centuries. They have become popular in modern times, partially due to the work of Dr. Edward Bach of England. In this method of healing, the underlying premise is that disease originates in the mind and emotions

## Treatment Methods and Traditional Remedies

before it is manifested in the body. Thus, by focusing on balancing thoughts and feelings, healing is effected at the physical level.

In the words of Dr. Bach, "The action of the flower essences raises the vibration of the being and opens up channels for the reception of the spiritual Self. They cure, not by attacking disease, but by flooding the being with the particular virtue needed, and washing out that which is causing harm. Like beautiful music or any glorious uplifting thing which gives us inspiration, they are able to raise our very natures. They provide creative patterns of harmony that bring us nearer to our souls, and by that very act, bring us peace and relieve our suffering. They cure by flooding the body with the beautiful vibrations of the highest nature – in whose presence there is the opportunity for disease to melt away like snow in sunshine."

Flower essence of Tulasi has many therapeutic properties. It is commonly used to treat fear and lack of faith. It is renowned for its ability to remove disease, sadness and suffering. It cultivates devotion, harmony and trust.

Place two to three drops in water. Take this two to three times a day. As flower essences work on a very subtle level, it is best to take them on a regular basis for at least several weeks. Flower essences can also be used externally in a mist or bath to purify the subtle body.

## Traditional Remedies: Tulasi Water, Juice, Powder and Paste

For those taking Tulasi preventatively, eating one leaf a day is sufficient. People with health conditions usually ingest larger quantities of the plant.

In traditional Indian society, one custom is for women to worship and offer prayers to the Tulasi plant early every morning. While this method is practised as a spiritual ritual, there is a medicinal reason for it as well. It has been observed that in the early morning, the Tulasi plant releases ozone ($O_3$). Inhaling these vapours has been proven to be extremely beneficial for the female reproductive system, as well as overall immunity and health.

Ancient ayurvedic texts outline a vast number of treatments using Tulasi. Its seeds can be used to treat dysuria (inhibited ability to urinate), parasites, debility and diarrhoea. The juice is known as *amapacana,* meaning 'that which digests and destroys *ama*, or toxicity'. Made into a paste, Tulasi works well against ringworm when

## Treatment Methods and Traditional Remedies

applied topically. Making a pulp from the leaves and applying it as an external dressing stops infections and accelerates healing. Chewing Tulasi leaves helps with ulcers, mouth infections and gum diseases. Placing fresh leaf juice in the ear has been known to heal even the most chronic ear infections.

Tulasi leaves or powder mixed with ginger and black pepper, sweetened with jaggery (raw cane sugar) or honey is an especially beneficial treatment for boosting immunity and reducing mucous in conditions such as bronchitis, asthma, influenza, coughs and colds. This is a well-known remedy in Southern India, and is used by many people at Amma's ashram.

During the rainy season, when malaria and dengue fever are prevalent in some parts of Asia, Tulasi leaves act as a preventative and treatment for these diseases. A decoction of Tulasi leaves, powdered cardamom, jaggery and pure quality milk reduces fever. The juice of Tulasi leaves can also be used for this purpose.

Tulasi has a nourishing and strengthening effect on the kidneys. In case of renal stones, regular intake of Tulasi leaf juice with honey can help to expel them via the urinary tract.

Tulasi has a beneficial effect on cholesterol levels and treats cardiac disease. Additionally, it has a positive effect on blood pressure and regular use may help to prevent heart attacks. A tonic can be prepared by mixing one gram of dry Tulasi leaves with a spoonful of ghee and honey.

Tulasi is an excellent remedy for headaches. A decoction of leaves and water can be taken several times until there is relief. Pounded leaves, sandalwood paste and chickweed powder applied to the forehead, bring immediate relief from excessive heat and headache.

Tulasi is also an effective ingredient in many body care products, such as salves, lotions, massage oils, facial masks, creams, pastes, etc. Due to its antibacterial properties, it is excellent for the skin.

# Chapter 4

# Botany

Tulasi is botanically termed as *Ocimum sanctum* L. It was later renamed *Ocimum tenuiflorum* L., although this synonym is rarely used. The two varieties of *Ocimum sanctum* are commonly called Krishna Tulasi and Rama Tulasi. *Ocimum sanctum* is indigenous to India, Afghanistan, Pakistan, and tropical Asia.

Tulasi belongs to the *Lamiaceae/Labiatae* Family and to the Genus *Ocimum*. It is a close relative of *Ocimum basilicum,* the well-known culinary basil. Tulasi is commonly referred to as Holy Basil in English. The Tulasi being discussed in this book is *Ocimum sanctum.*

There are other closely related plants referred to as varieties of Tulasi that do not carry the same level of medicinal potency as *Ocimum sanctum.* Vana Tulasi, or *Ocimum gratissimum,* is one such example. Vana Tulasi grows wild in many areas of Asia, North and Eastern Africa, and is widely cultivated throughout South East Asia.

## Description

Tulasi is an upright, many-branched herbaceous shrub, which can grow from a half-metre to one and a half metres in height. The oval-shaped

leaves are pointed at the tip, between two to four centimetres in length and display different hues of green and purple, depending on the variety. Rama Tulasi varies from bright to dark green.

Krishna varieties can range from green with purple edges and stems to fully dark purple. When Krishna Tulasi and Rama Tulasi plants are grown in close proximity, they will cross-pollinate. The next generation of plants will be a blend of the two, with the green shades often dominating.

With more sunlight, the purple shades become more pronounced. All of Tulasi's inflorescents, or flowering stalks, are long and thin with tiny whorls of light purple flowers.

Vana Tulasi has bright, light-green leaves, and white flowers. While the leaves of Rama and Krishna are highly aromatic with a slightly clove-like smell, Vana Tulasi has a distinct lemony fragrance and taste. For this reason, Vana Tulasi is often used in combination with Krishna and Rama Tulasi in teas.

## Constituents

Tulasi contains a complex volatile oil, comprised partially of eugenol. This is the active constituent that has been found to be largely responsible for its therapeutic potentials (59). It also contains methyl eugenol, caryophyllene, triterpenoid ursolic acid, oleanic acid and rosmarinic acid, amongst other components. The fixed oil found within the *Ocimum sanctum* seeds contains five fatty acids (stearic, palmitic, oleic, linoleic and linolenic acids) which demonstrate significant anti-inflammatory benefits (6).

## Common Names of Tulasi in Various Languages

The names of *Ocimum sanctum* are in bold; the other names refer to either *Ocimum sanctum,* or other closely related varieties in the *Ocimum* Genus (87)(88)(89).
Arabic: Dohsh, Schadjant, Vasub

*Botany*

Assamese: **Tulasii**
Bengali: Kalatulsi, **Kalotulsi**, Kural, **Tulsi**, Tulshi
Burmese: **Laun**, Pinsein-net, Kala-pinsein
Chinese: **Sheng luó lè**
Dutch: **Heilig Basilicum**
English: **Holy Basil, Sacred Basil**
Finnish: Pyhä basilika
French: Basilic Sacré
German: **Heiliges Basilikum**, Indisches Basilikum
Gujarati: **Tulsi, Talasi**
Hindi: **Tulsi**, Baranda, Kalatulsi, **Krishnatulsi**, Varanda, Jangalii tulasii
Indonesian: **Lampes, Ruku-Ruku**
Italian: Basilico Sacro
Japanese: **Kami mebouki**
Kannada: Kalatulsi, Karitulasi, **Shri Tulasi, Tulasi, Vishnu Tulasi**
Kanarese: Kalatulsi, Karitulasi, Sritulasi, Tulasi
Khmer: **Mrea preu**
Laotian: **Saphaa**, Sa phao lom deng, Sa phao lom khao, Phak i tou thai
Lithuanian: **Siauralapis bazilikas**
Malay: Kemangi, Selasih merah, Selasih Siam, **Oku, Ruku-ruku, Sulasi**

*Tulasi Devi,* the Goddess of Devotion

Malayalam: **Tulasi, Krishnatulasi**, Kunnakam, Punya, **Shivatulasi, Shri Tulasi, Trittavu, Pachchatulasi**
Marathi: **Tulasa**
Nepalese: Krishna, Tulsii Maa, **Tulasii Patra**
Oriya: Dhalatulasi
Punjabi: **Tulsi**
Sanskrit: Ajaka, Arjaka, Brinda (Vrinda), Gauri, Gramya, Haripriya, Krishnamula, **Krishna Tulasi,** Lakshmi, Madhavi, Manjari, Madurutala, Mudura tulla, Parnasa, Patrapuspha, Sri Tulasi, Suvasa, **Tulasi, Tulasii,** Vaishnavi, Vishnupriya.
Singhalese: **Madurutala,** Madura tulla
Spanish: Sagrado Basilico
Tagalog: **Loko-loko**
Tamil: Alungai, Karut Tulasi, Kullai, Nalla Thulasi, **Tiruttizhai, Tiruttilai, Tulasi**
Thai: **Kapao**, Kaprao, Kom Ko Dong
Telugu: Tulsichettu, **Tulasi, Krishnatulasi**, Brynda, gaggera, **Oddhi**
Urdu: **Janglitulsi**, Kali Tulsi, **Tulsi**
Vietnamese: E rung, **Nhu tía**, **É do**

## Chapter 5

# Growing Tulasi Throughout the World

## GreenFriends Distribution of Tulasi

GreenFriends, Amma's environmental initiative, emphasises love and respect for Mother Nature with an awareness of our duty to protect Her. GreenFriends encourages the reawakening of the ancient traditions that revere Mother Nature, particularly recommending the practice of daily worship of Tulasi as a way to cultivate awareness of the divinity within Nature. To facilitate this practice and to promote the many healing benefits of Tulasi, GreenFriends groups grow Tulasi plants across North America, Europe, Japan and Australia. Many people from around the world participate in the process of learning to cultivate Tulasi in non-native climates. The following information details their shared experiences. Amma also has given specific guidance on the growing process.

## *Tulasi Devi,* the Goddess of Devotion

When GreenFriends first started distributing Tulasi seeds internationally, a few loving gardeners brought their baby plants to the first programme of Amma's annual North American tour. Seattle, Washington, known for its foggy, cold weather, happened to be where GreenFriends received their first batch of Tulasi seedlings. Unfortunately, the difficulty of growing Tulasi in a temperate climate quickly became apparent. A compassionate would-be adopter of one particularly weak plant decided to take it to Amma. After seeing the condition of the sad little seedling, Amma lovingly stressed the importance of carefully instructing each individual on how to grow these plants. Amma remarked that Rama Tulasi might be a little easier to grow in colder areas, as Krishna Tulasi seems to prefer stronger sunlight. Amma suggested that people in colder areas could grow Tulasi indoors by a sunny, slightly humid window.

Even with the difficulties of growing Tulasi in colder areas, Amma enthusiastically encouraged GreenFriends to continue cultivating it throughout the world. We have experienced that the extra love and nurturing these plants require can help people to grow as well.

## Growing Tulasi Throughout the World

As this journey of learning continued, our knowledge of caring for the Tulasi plants grew. Year after year, people have shared unique stories about growing Tulasi. Some have seen their Tulasi plants grow like wild even in extremely cold areas, such as a woman from snowy Wisconsin, whose beloved Tulasi thrived for years by a sunny window. Others had trouble just sprouting the seeds, even in places such as sunny Los Angeles. Tulasi is considered a perennial in tropical climates, living in some areas for up to five years under normal circumstances. In temperate climates, She would be considered an annual, living for one season or a year. Nevertheless, with proper care and a little grace, many people are able to grow their Tulasi for several years.

One GreenFriend discovered an innovative way to grow hundreds of vibrant Tulasi plants that he brings every year to Amma's annual November programs in Michigan. The plants, although in small pots, are uniquely shaped and maturely developed, in a manner similar to the Japanese art of bonsai trees. Many of his methods are the basis of this growing section. Amma was delighted with his ability to grow such strong and beautiful Tulasi plants, especially during the snowy winter

## *Tulasi Devi,* the Goddess of Devotion

in Michigan. Remarking on how this technique strengthened the root structures of the plants, Amma suggested that he share his methods with everyone interested in growing Tulasi in temperate climates. When he brought a new batch the following year, Amma revealed that these Tulasi plants were growing so well due to the love and devotion with which he cared for them. This is a testimony to the power of love, as most people find it very difficult to grow Tulasi in such a cold, snowy place.

There is no doubt that Tulasi, like all other plants, responds profoundly to our love. Nonetheless, the process of loving and learning to grow Tulasi has seen many plants grow and die. If a Tulasi doesn't make it, it is not necessarily due to a lack of love or effort. When a plant returns to the soil, it nurtures a new beginning. There are plenty of new seeds awaiting the chance to awaken and grow.

Amma expressed how wonderful it was to see so many people caring for their newly acquired baby Tulasi plants. More than once, She shared that through the experience of taking these sacred plants home and nurturing them, love for Mother Nature awakens in people's hearts. Thus, one of the purposes in distributing the Tulasi seeds was revealed to be the reawakening of reverence for Mother Nature.

## How to Grow Tulasi

### Getting Started: Materials Needed for Seedlings

Investing in a few inexpensive items will definitely make the growing process easier, especially if you live in a colder climate. However, there are many options if you wish to avoid purchasing new items; soil can be prepared at home, old trays, pots and other materials can be collected or recycled, and so forth. A basic list is given below and detailed information is outlined throughout the chapter.

• Organic seedling soil mix, store-bought or home-made (See recipe in the Soil and Nutrition section.)

• A seedling flat with individual plugs (sections), peat moss cups or other small, individual containers. (Peat moss cups can be directly transplanted into larger containers later on, with no disturbance to the babies. If you wish to recycle, simply wash used plastic cups and poke holes in

*Tulasi Devi,* the Goddess of Devotion

the bottom. Whatever you choose to use should be at least two inches deep.)
- A fitted, clear plastic dome, lid or glass to cover your tray or pots.
- For locations with inadequate sunlight, two or more florescent full-spectrum tube light bulbs (Ask for a shop light fixture for the bulbs.)
- For locations where temperatures are too low for germination, a heating mat for seeds can be used.

**Materials You Will Need as Your Plants Grow**

- Organic potting soil (Store bought is the easiest and has the best combination of nutrients for your plant. If you already have a garden and want to make your own, see the recipe in Soil and Nutrition section.)
- Organic fertiliser such as compost, dried or composted cow manure, worm castings or worm casting tea, or a store-bought, organic fertiliser specifically for the 'growth stage'
- Pots for transplanting as your plant grows
- Light (See Sunlight and Indoor Light section for details.)
- Water (preferably filtered)
- Love!

## Invocation Ritual

It is always nice to start off with a small ritual or prayer to assist the growth of the seeds. You can use the one below, which is used in Amma's ashram, or create your own.

Imagine planting seeds of devotion in the soil of your heart that you will nurture every day with awareness and love. Place your hands on the soil after planting. Close your eyes and intone the sacred syllable *AUM*. In *Sanatana Dharma* (Hinduism), *AUM* is considered the primordial sound vibration of creation. As you intone *AUM,* visualise the vibration awakening the life-force energy in the seeds. With the second *AUM*, imagine the seed starting to sprout and grow. With the third *AUM,* you can visualise the plant fully-grown, lush and vibrant!

You can also chant traditional prayers (*mantras*) for peace, Tulasi mantras, or any other personal prayers or songs. Feel free to adapt this ritual in any way you feel inspired. A tangible feeling of harmony is created by doing this ritual in groups. It is also a fun and inspiring practice to share with children, as they readily love to use the power of their imagination. The *AUM* ritual can also be chanted after transplanting, while placing your hands around the base of plant, as the soothing vibrations reduce transplant shock.

**Planting with the Moon**

Ancient cultures have long utilised the effect that the lunar phases have on the growth of plants. Just as the moon pulls the tides in the oceans, it also pulls upon other subtle bodies of water, causing moisture to rise in the earth, which encourages growth. These same forces create more water in the soil at the time of the new and full moon. This increased moisture encourages the seeds to sprout and grow. The optimal period for harvesting, transplanting and pruning is the two weeks after the full moon when the light is waning. During the new moon, and up until the moon is full, is the ideal time for sowing seeds.

**Soil and Nutrition**

Give Tulasi a light, fertile and well-draining soil. It is best to buy organic seedling soil mix and organic potting soil from your local nursery. It is important to choose organic soil, as this will contribute to the overall health of the Tulasi, the purity and medicinal potency of the leaves and the harmony of Mother Nature. Non-organic blends contain toxic chemical fertilisers that contaminate the plants and pollute the environment. Take the time to carefully read the labels and avoid those containing chemical fertilisers.

If Her leaves start to turn yellow and drop, it may also be a sign that your Tulasi is lacking nitrogen in Her soil. Nitrogen is a key nutrient essential to healthy plant growth. Once a month, give your Tulasi a little home-made compost, worm castings (vermicompost), or cow manure that is either well-composted, aged or dried. Alternatively, you can make a fertiliser by diluting one part aged cow manure or compost in three parts water. Water with this once every two weeks. Sprinkle a little wood ash on the leaves and around the base of the plant to provide potassium. This helps to keep Tulasi plants healthy and green. Generally, Tulasi will need more nutrients in warmer weather when She grows more, and will need less in colder months.

Always take care not to overdo fertilisers, as too high a dose of nitrogen or other nutrients can 'burn' the plant, causing young leaves to get black spots and die or wilt, even with sufficient watering. If this happens, wash out the excess nutrients by flushing the soil continuously with water and allowing it to drain out from the bottom.

If you prefer to make your own potting soil or seedling soil mix rather than purchasing it, try the following recipes:

**Potting Soil Mix**

- One part organic compost, well decomposed and sifted
- One part salt-free coarse river sand (for added drainage)
- Two parts healthy garden soil (Look for dark soil with a bit of humus; it should form a ball for a few moments if squeezed together.)
- A small quantity of peat moss, vermiculite or perlite (optional)

**Seedling Soil Mix**

- One part well-sifted compost
- One part potting soil or healthy garden soil
- Two parts salt-free coarse river sand
- A small amount of peat moss, vermiculite or perlite (optional)
- Seedling soil mix should be fine and light with very good drainage.

## Planting Seeds

Tulasi seeds are amazingly minuscule. They require extra attention and care while planting due to their delicate size. Use store bought organic seedling soil mix or prepare it at home with the above recipe.

Fill seedling flats, peat moss cups, or small individual containers with seedling soil mix. Place the tray or containers in a larger tray of water, allowing the soil to absorb the water from below for at least several hours before planting. Avoid watering from overhead, as this compacts the soil and can misplace the tiny seeds. Gently press the seeds into the surface of the soil. If you cannot find a tray with individual plugs, plant the seeds every inch, in rows two-square inches apart from each other. When using individual containers, plant one or two seeds per container. If two sprout, you will later need to thin the plants to one per container.

There are two methods in seeding that work well. Feel free to try either one or both. The first method is to lay your seeds on top, pressing them slightly into the soil (to protect them from drying out) and keeping them uncovered. The alternative method is to sprinkle a little soil on top of the seeds with a sifter (such as a flour sifter

## *Tulasi Devi,* the Goddess of Devotion

or powdered sugar sifter) to ensure the top layer stays thin and fine. Make sure the soil on top is only equal, in depth, to the diameter of the tiny seed. In many cases, Tulasi seeds take much longer to germinate or do not germinate at all if they become buried too far beneath the surface of the soil. Use a spray bottle and water with a mist, as the fine water droplets will not dislodge the seeds or disturb the new-born plants.

It is ideal to place a clear plastic dome on top of the tray or containers. Planting trays with fitted plastic domes are usually available from an indoor gardening store. If you cannot get one, use a piece of clear plastic, a clear plastic bag, or a piece of clear glass. This will create the warm and humid atmosphere in which the seeds love to sprout. Leave a small gap for ventilation (using small stones, sticks or other props) and be sure to check that the temperature does not get too hot under the plastic or glass. The amount of ventilation needed will depend on how hot it is.

Place your seedlings in a very warm or sunny place. The ideal temperature is at least a steady 80° Fahrenheit or 26° Celsius. In colder conditions, you may need a seed heating mat (available in indoor gardening stores) or a full-spectrum lamp (see Sunlight and Indoor Light section) to help your little seeds sprout. Lower or inconsistent temperatures will cause the seeds to take longer to germinate. Tulasi will not germinate at all if the temperature is consistently too low. If you really want to get creative, you can place a two-inch layer of fresh horse manure under the trays, as this generates bottom heat. Horse manure is known as 'hot' manure, meaning it heats as it breaks down.

Tulasi seeds normally sprout within five to seven days, but can take up to five weeks or even longer, depending on the temperature and other factors. Some of the seeds may sprout sooner than others. In most cases, seedlings can continue to appear over a few weeks. The baby plants first emerge with two tiny bright leaves that have slightly rounded tips and are almost square at the corners. These are called the cotyledons, or the leaves fed by the seed. As they develop, a single root pushes down into the soil, also fed by the energy in the seed. After a few days, as their tiny roots develop, they acquire a second set of two more leaves. These are the first true leaves, which are fed by the soil through the newly developed roots and sunlight.

## *Tulasi Devi,* the Goddess of Devotion

If using a plastic dome, leave it in place until the seedlings reach the top. If the weather is still cold as the plants grow larger, experiment with making a mini-greenhouse, using a frame and clear plastic. The soil should always be kept slightly moist, but never too wet or soggy. Maintain good drainage at all times, as too much moisture in the soil can cause the seedlings to begin 'damp-

ing off'. This is a condition in which the bottom of the stem rots from a fungus.

If the seedlings are growing together in a tray, wait until their third set of leaves sprouts before transplanting. If the seedlings are grown in their own tiny pots, then they can be left until their roots are actively growing out of the bottom of the

## Growing Tulasi Throughout the World

container before being transplanted. If you have used peat moss cups for your seedlings, simply place the full cup into a larger pot filled with soil and water.

### Transplanting Baby Tulasi Plants

If Tulasi is started in a tray without individual sections, you will need to carefully transplant the babies into their own little pots. The idea to hold firmly in mind whenever transplanting is that Tulasi will not even know that She is being moved. Imagine lifting a sleeping child, wrapped in her baby blanket, from the couch to a bed. If the blanket falls off, she may wake up. Likewise, keep the blanket of original soil around the roots when moving the baby Tulasi. Use a spoon to scoop as much soil as you can around the roots without disturbing the other babies. Avoid letting soil fall off, which may expose fragile, new roots to the air and light. Make a small hole with your fingertips in Her new home, matching the size of Her roots and soil. Be sure to match the soil level at the stem to the same level it was in the seeding tray. Planting Her too high or too low can cause damage. If needed, adjust the size of the hole before laying Her in a new bed. Try not to disturb Her by crushing Her delicate roots down to fit into a hole that is too small or by dropping Her into a hole that is too deep. Give your Tulasi baby extra water before and after relocating Her. If possible, keep freshly transplanted babies in the shade for one full day.

If you find the Tulasi babies grew very close together in the tray, try to gently ease their roots apart as carefully as possible. Hold the baby plants at the base of their stems while gently pulling back and forth to untangle their roots. Do your best to keep the soil intact. If they have become extremely entangled, separate them using room temperature water, and plant them immediately.

Before transplanting out of plug trays or individual containers, make sure the roots have fully filled the plug and are growing slightly out of the bottom. Water thoroughly and gently pull from the base of the stem, slowly easing it out. Slipping a butter knife around the inside of the container will assist in lifting the seedling out gently. If it is not sliding out, do not pull harder. Simply give more water and try again.

### Transplanting into Larger Pots

As Tulasi continues to grow, She will gradually need more space. You will know She is ready to be transplanted when Her roots begin to grow thickly out of the bottom of the container. It is best to replant into a new container that is one inch bigger in diameter on all sides. She should never be moved to a pot much bigger than Her current one. The excess soil in the new pot could retain more water than the plant can utilise, causing potential root damage.

Place a few small stones on the bottom of the pot to ensure the drainage holes do not get blocked. Fill the new pot partially with potting

## *Tulasi Devi*, the Goddess of Devotion

soil. Bear in mind that the new soil level should be the same as the original soil level. If the soil is higher, it can rot the bottom stem of the Tulasi; if it is too low, it can expose the roots. Water the new pot of soil and the Tulasi plant thoroughly. You may need to use a knife to slide around the edges of the original pot to loosen the earth. Keeping your hand around the base of the plant, tip over the pot and tap gently. She should slide out without much trouble. If you are having trouble, do not force the plant out; instead, give more water to loosen the soil. Your Tulasi may also have difficulty sliding out if the roots have not grown fully into the pot.

After giving Tulasi water to help Her settle into Her new home, place Her in the shade for a full day. Transplanting in the late afternoon is preferable in hotter climates, as the cool evening helps the plants to adjust. As your Tulasi gets bigger and heavier, you may need a friend to assist you in the transplanting process.

### Shaping and Plucking Tulasi for Optimum Health

Tulasi has an active growing point at the tip of Her stem, causing Her to grow straight upwards until the growth point develops into a flower bud. If you allow the Tulasi to grow too long before picking the top of Her stem, She may become leggy or top-heavy. When your young Tulasi reaches about eight to ten inches in height, gently pluck Her

top set of leaves. From this point, She will begin to branch out, forming two stems where there was previously one. When each of the new branches has developed three or four sets of leaves, or when they create their first flower bud, gently pluck the tip. This will encourage two more shoots to start on that branch. When the branching system is supported in this way, Tulasi produces a full and healthy growth structure. The process of plucking Tulasi's tips strengthens and thickens Her main stalk, and sends more energy into the roots for a stronger support system.

The larger, older leaves become less effective at photosynthesis, and are eventually dropped off by

## *Tulasi Devi,* the Goddess of Devotion

the plant. As they begin to droop, they should also be picked. This further encourages new growth, sending the energy of the plant into the tiny new leaves at the apex of the stem and larger leaf. When removing the larger leaves, pluck gently at the rounded base of the leaf, leaving intact the tiny stem that connects it to the larger stem.

It may be necessary to prop your Tulasi up with a thin stake for extra support. This will help Her to grow straight until Her stem becomes thicker and woodier. Try to pick only a few leaves a day per plant. You can eat the leaves. However, never over-pick your Tulasi if She is too young, small or weak.

Once, two young girls brought a large, fully flowering Tulasi to Amma and asked Her advice about how to care for it. Amma asked them to pluck the flowers using their fingers, as the Tulasi would be afraid of cutting tools. In this case, it is helpful to have sharp nails! In rare circumstances in which a thicker part of the plant needs to be removed, it may be necessary to use a cutting tool.

## Flower and Seed Collecting

It is important to pluck flowering buds as soon as they appear, as most of Tulasi's growing energy is used to produce the flowers. A healthy Tulasi that receives sufficient sunlight will generally flower continuously. Tiny, light purple blossoms form in small clusters along a thin stalk. The bottom clusters bloom first and then continue to open up as they rise to the tip.

Tulasi's flowers are called *manjaris* in Sanskrit, and are considered to be an auspicious offering in some branches of Hindu worship. Other Hindu traditions offer only the leaves and never the flowers.

If you wish to allow the flowers to grow past the bud stage, be sure to collect them when they are new and soft, before they mature into tiny seed pods. This process, known as 'going to seed', takes a lot of the vitality from the plant.

On the other hand, if you wish to collect seeds, wait until your Tulasi becomes fully-grown and healthy. At that time, allow only a few flowers at a time to mature into seed pods. When the flowers drop, you will notice their base turn green and mature into a delicate shell-like structure encasing four tiny white seeds. Wait for the entire flower stalk to become brown and dry and for the seeds inside to turn dark brown, then collect the seeds.

Store the seeds in a small brown paper bag and keep it in a cool, dark and dry place. If you do not gather them first, the seeds will fall out of their shell. Under ideal conditions, these seeds can sometimes sprout at the base of the original plant. However, the Tulasi seeds are a favourite treat for ants, so try to collect them before they fall, or they may be eaten. They may also dry out if they fall and go unnoticed. If you missed a few seeds, you may still be lucky enough for some to sprout on their own. Carefully move the new babies as soon as they have two leaves, without disturbing the roots of the mother plant.

Amma reminded us on many occasions that it is important to allow the Tulasi seeds to breathe.

*Growing Tulasi Throughout the World*

Once when She saw the seeds we packed in small, sealed plastic bags, She suggested that we poke a hole in the packets using a needle. This way, the seeds would receive some air.

On one occasion, Amma lovingly gazed at a clear packet of Tulasi seeds and playfully shook them back and forth. She said, *"The little seeds are*

*speaking with each other. They are asking, 'Where will we go? Who will take care of us? Where will we be planted?'"* Certainly there is no doubting the consciousness in these magical little seeds! Then, Amma recalled a touching story She had once told about a Tulasi seed and a Lotus seed. The story was set in the enchanting time of Lord Krishna and His beloved gopis. The Tulasi seed played a symbolic role, conveying a profound teaching of how limits can be overcome in order to grow closer to the Divine. Amma, in a childlike way, shared that this sweet story had come from Her imagination. This story has been included in Chapter 8, exactly as Amma narrated it.

**Finding the Right Home for Your Tulasi Plant**

When choosing the ideal place for your Tulasi, vital factors to consider are light and heat. If you live in a warm, humid climate, it is best to grow the Tulasi outdoors in full sunlight during the warmer months. Tulasi thrives in such a climate, and may suffer indoors if exposed to air-conditioning or insufficient light and humidity. However, make sure to bring Her indoors before the weather drops below 50°F or 10°C. Although Tulasi can survive in colder weather, Her growth may considerably slow down if temperatures drop any lower than this.

Tulasi may be grown indoors in climates that are not so hot and humid, or if there is not adequate outdoor space. When growing Tulasi inside, be careful to protect Her from air-conditioning, and follow the instructions given in the section on proper lighting conditions. Always ensure that your Tulasi is placed in such a way as to have good ventilation and drainage.

If you grow Tulasi indoors during the winter, and want to relocate Her outdoors in the spring, do so gradually. Otherwise, it is actually possible for the leaves to get 'burnt' and for the Tulasi to go into shock from a rapid change in environment. One sign of this would be the leaves turning yellow and dropping suddenly. Slowly acclimatise Tulasi by bringing Her outside for a few hours each day. You can increase the duration daily as She adjusts.

## Sunlight and Indoor Light

When growing Tulasi indoors, your sunniest window will be the best place for Her. Tulasi needs at least three to six hours of direct sunlight daily, and as much indirect light as possible. Kitchen windows are often preferable as they usually provide additional humidity that benefits the plants. Take care to prevent any cold drafts from coming through the window at night. If this is not possible, you may need to move the Tulasi away from

## *Tulasi Devi,* the Goddess of Devotion

the window in the evening. When growing Tulasi near a window, it is a good idea to rotate the pot a little each day, as She will naturally grow towards the source of light. Receiving sunlight on all sides will encourage even growth.

If there is not enough sunlight and warmth coming in through a window in the colder months, it is best to use a full-spectrum florescent light. These light bulbs imitate the rays of natural sunlight. Full-spectrum tube lights are the least expensive source of light for growing plants indoors and they use the least electricity. You can purchase a 'shop light' fixture at any hardware store. Ask for two full-spectrum tube bulbs that fit into the fixture. You can find them, along with a variety of other full-spectrum lighting options, at indoor gardening centres.

In most cases, your plants will grow better with this additional light through the winter. Indoor light is also ideal to help get a head start by germinating seeds in the early spring. Keep the fixtures as close to Tulasi as possible. This light will not burn Her. The light will be inefficient and ineffective if located too far away, as Tulasi will grow long and leggy to reach it. Just before She touches the light, adjust the fixture a few inches higher. If indoor bulbs are your main light source, it is best to use more than one fixture, arranging them to provide light from all angles. The best arrangement is two fixtures on either side of Her, providing sufficient light for well-rounded growth. If the light source only comes from above, Her lower leaves and branches may not grow, resulting in a top-heavy plant with a weak stem.

When using only indoor lights with no other light source, leave them on for 14-16 hours a day. If you are still getting some direct sunlight, then you can supplement this with the additional indoor light. For example, if you get four hours of direct sunlight, you can leave the lights on for 10-12 additional hours.

You will know your Tulasi is not getting sufficient light if the leaf colour becomes pale, leaves drop, or stems and branches become weak and leggy. A sign of sufficient light is a strong, robust plant, vibrant with colour and lush growth of leaves.

It is not unusual for Tulasi to become less vibrant in the winter. Sometimes, She may even loose many of Her leaves. Do not give up hope! Simply continue to give Her as much warmth and light as possible. In most cases, Her vibrancy will return with the spring. Her bright, young leaves sprouting with a burst of new life offer an encouraging sign that you have made it through the winter together.

**Watering Your Tulasi**

It is best to water your Tulasi in the early morning or late afternoon. Watering when the sun is too strong can burn the leaves if the water droplets heat up. Also, the water may evaporate before fully nourishing your Tulasi. How often you water will depend on many factors, such as temperature, humidity and soil type. Light, well-draining soil is ideal. The soil should become slightly dry between each watering so that the roots get sufficient oxygen to breathe and grow. Waterlogged soil affects the health of the roots, causing fungus and disease. Over-watering can cause the leaves to become pale or yellow, or dry and brown at the edges. It can also cause them to drop from the plant.

Lightly press your fingertip about one-quarter inch into Tulasi's soil surface each day to feel if She needs water. If Her soil is still moist, give it a chance to dry before watering again. Be careful not to wait so long that the topsoil becomes hard and crusty and watch that the leaves do not become limp with thirst. Water gently with a spray nozzle hose or with a watering can. Avoid using a heavy force of water as it could expose the roots. If you notice the soil becoming compacted over time, use your fingers to aerate it by gently by turning the surface of the soil a little. Only turn the top inch, being careful not to disturb the roots.

Give Her a moderate amount of water for the soil to remain slightly moist throughout the day. Observing the weather each day is a good idea, as on very hot days she needs more water, and on cloudy days, She needs less. Approximately once a week, water deeply so that the water flows out of the drainage holes, flushing out any excess build-up of salts in the soil.

Remember that the rain is the best form of watering, and if possible, take the plant outside whenever it rains for an hour or two. Tulasi will be experiencing a communion with all the energies of rain, which offer Her more than water alone.

In India, there is a common belief that all plants sleep at night. This conviction reflects the close association between plants and humanity. Amma is often given Tulasi, as well as other plants. She frequently kisses them and sometimes holds them up to Her head in reverence, as a gesture

## Tulasi Devi, the Goddess of Devotion

of bowing to the plant. During one of Amma's evening programmes, someone brought a Tulasi plant to Amma as an offering. After receiving the Tulasi, Amma gently handed Her to a girl who then, rather awkwardly, set Her down with a loud

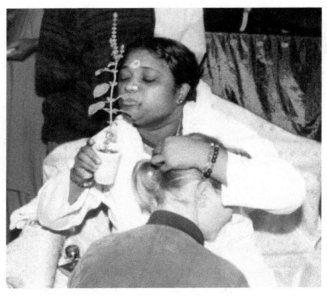

bump. In the tone of a mother feeling protective of her sleeping baby, Amma softly exclaimed, *"Oh no, you woke Her up!"* With this awareness, you may want to avoid watering, picking or otherwise unnecessarily disturbing your Tulasi at night.

## Providing Sufficient Humidity

Tulasi loves humidity. If you live in a dry, arid climate, you may need to find creative ways to increase Tulasi's moisture intake through Her leaves. Dry air can cause Her leaves to curl and turn brown at the edges. In such conditions, She may also look thirsty, even if you have been giving Her adequate water. Misting water on the leaves with a spray bottle increases humidity. Placing two or more pots of Tulasi together can help, as the plants will enjoy sharing the moisture that they transpire. A little greenhouse can be created by covering a dome or frame with clear plastic and placing it over the plant. This will trap the humidity and heat inside. However, be careful not to allow excessive heat to build up, and remove the plastic if necessary. You can also put water and gravel or sponge rock in a tray. Then, set Tulasi on top of the rocks, ensuring that the water level is below the pot.

## Pests and Diseases

Keeping your Tulasi plant strong and healthy is a main priority, as pests and diseases tend to attack weaker plants. Another important factor is careful daily observation of your Tulasi plant.

## *Tulasi Devi,* the Goddess of Devotion

If discovered early, pests and diseases are usually easy to address. However, if these first signs are overlooked, they can rapidly develop into a larger problem. This can be compared to the daily practice of observing our mind and making the effort to transcend any negative thoughts before they take root. Likewise, to nurture the growth of positive virtues within, we should not allow ourselves to be overtaken by the pests of negativities.

Care for your Tulasi plant by daily removing leaves that look old and sick. Rinse Her daily with a gentle mist from a spray bottle or hose, paying special attention to the underside of Her leaves, where bugs often gather. Once a week, give Her a bath, this time using a spray bottle of diluted soapy water, followed after ten minutes by a rinse of plain water. Use castile soaps, and avoid getting the soapy water into Her roots by tipping Her at an angle. Having a few ladybugs around is always a good idea, as these little ladies like to feast on many of the pests that eat up Tulasi. Other beneficial insects include the praying mantis, lacewings and ambush bugs.

Plants that feed in well-balanced, organic soil utilise exactly what they need from a myriad of nutrients, including trace elements. This nourishment produces a healthy, balanced plant, enabling it to produce pheromones that repel insects and diseases. The basis of organic farming is feeding the plants from the soil, versus from the water in the soil. This requires carbon in the form of humus, or composted organic matter, in the soil. Humus has the quality of bonding mineral nutrients in a relatively non-leachable manner. It also hosts bacteria that help enable the plant roots to absorb these nutrients. Chemical fertilisers are soluble. The plants are forced to receive these soluble nutrients in the water. However, they do not have the ability to separate out the nutrients that they need. This results in the absorption of excess nutrients, which will weaken the plants. Weaker plants are more susceptible to pests and diseases.

## *Spider mites*

Hot and dry weather may bring along the appearance of tiny green or yellow dots on the leaves. This is a sign that your Tulasi may have spider mites. Although the spider mites are practically invisible, at an acute stage, you will see their fine webbing. As these insects suck the sap of the leaves, the leaf tissue is destroyed, becoming dry, pale yellow and brown at the tips. Whole sections of the plant may even wither. The tiny mites live on the underside of Her leaves and lay small white eggs next to the veins of the leaf. Regular soapy baths are needed. Swish your whole Tulasi plant gently in a bucket of soapy water, holding Her carefully and protecting Her soil with plastic around the base. Rinse Her off with a strong spray angled to get underneath Her leaves. Be certain it is strong enough to spray off the mites without damaging the plant. For larger infestations, mix one-quarter teaspoon of neem oil, or other pyrethrin oils, and one-half teaspoon of soap in one quart of water and spray. Other types of natural sprays can be purchased at a gardening store. Follow the instructions carefully, and always avoid chemical sprays, as they weaken the plant, harm your health and damage the environment. Keeping your Tulasi out of the late afternoon sun or arid weather will also help to reduce the spider mite infestation.

## *Aphids*

Aphids are tiny flea-shaped mites; varying in colour from black to green or yellow. They crowd together on the underside of leaves and slowly

## Growing Tulasi Throughout the World

suck the sap. They can be hard to detect in the beginning, as the leaves will continue to appear healthy for some time. However, they will eventually become yellow and drop, or become deformed or curly. For this reason, it is important to check the underside of your Tulasi's leaves often. When spotted, the first remedy is to remove a highly infested leaf. Leaves with fewer mites can be washed off with soapy water. A close eye must be kept on the plant for signs of re-infestation. The aphids multiply at an incredible rate, and an unspotted infestation can quickly get out of control. If the aphids drop, ants are likely to carry them and put them back on the plant. Ants and aphids are good friends. If you spot many ants on your plants, take a closer look, as this can be a sign of aphids. Unfortunately, the ants are not eating the aphids. They are actually 'farming' them. This means they are protecting the aphids and feeding off the sweet juices that the aphids secrete.

For serious infestations, or when there are many plants, we have discovered an excellent spray. Soak 200 grams of loose tobacco leaves in one litre of water for a day. Add 100 grams of cayenne chilli powder and 100 grams of fresh minced garlic. Soak for about three hours. Strain with a fine sifter. Dilute in a ratio of one part solution to four parts water. Use this in a spray bottle and be sure to reach the underside of the plants. Be careful not to allow any of the concoction to get into the soil. This mixture must be used up within two days, as the volatile oils from the garlic and chilli will become less effective.

Although this method is very successful, it is not recommended unless the other methods have failed. Also, avoid using this treatment more than once in a relatively short period of time. It is very strong, and excessive application can be detrimental to the growth of the plant. Always test this solution, seeking the weakest possible dilution that will effectively get rid of the aphids without damaging the plant. Spray in the late afternoon as midday sun heats the solution causing unnecessary damage to the plant. Ladybugs are helpful to have around, as they eat aphids.

### Ants

The biggest problem does not lie just with ants, but with the little friends they bring along with them. Ants 'farm' not only aphids, but mealy bugs and scales as well. They can actually carry pests from plant to plant, giving them protection and feasting on their secretions at the expense of the Tulasi. As mentioned earlier, ants will devour Tulasi seeds before they can mature on the plant or fall to the earth and sprout. Make sure your planting area is free from ants. If they are around, keeping the seedling flats on a table with each leg in a cup of water will solve the problem. In rare cases, ants can build a nest in the Tulasi pot, interfering with root growth. You can disturb the nest by giving a thorough watering, while providing a stick for the ants to use as a bridge to escape the flood. A few drops of peppermint essential oil in a spray bottle has been known to ward ants off. Ants also dislike salt, turmeric and cinnamon, although we have not found these to be consistently effective deterrents.

### Mealy bugs

If you spot a tiny, powdery white ball, you are actually seeing a soft-bodied bug whose many legs are covered in a cottony-looking substance. The bugs collect on the stems, crevices in the branch, and on the young leaves near the flowers. They will eventually suck away at Tulasi's sap. As they are easy to spot, the first remedy is to simply rub them off, or remove them with a forceful spray of soapy water. Keep a close eye, as they are likely to reappear, but will eventually die off if the population is kept in check. Neem oil or Sun Spray oil can also be applied.

## *Whiteflies*

Whiteflies are most likely to show up when the weather is humid and hot. Their name describes their appearance, although they are smaller than a common fly. They reproduce quickly and can be hard to control. The waxy clusters of babies cause the most trouble, sucking Tulasi's juice from the underside of the leaves. Neem, or sprays containing pyrethrum or soap, can diminish the adults, but the babies may need to be forcefully sprayed or wiped off the leaves. During the summer, a spray regime every five days is required for fighting an infestation. Yellow sticky traps specifically for whiteflies can also be purchased. *Encarsia formosa*, a small wasp, and *Delphastus pusillus*, a small black ladybird beetle will both help to control whiteflies.

## *Scales*

Scales look a bit like they sound. They are small, oval-shaped brown bumps that usually form on the branches. These are actually shells covering an insect. They can be gently scraped off as soon as they appear. Apply diluted neem oil or soapy water to the branch after scraping to discourage any unseen eggs from hatching.

### *Other Pests*

A stem borer that gets inside the stem and eats its way along can cause the unexpected wilting of an entire branch. The whole stem should be clipped to avoid the spread of the stem borer.

Leaf miners and other kinds of worms can live inside a leaf and feed on it. They chew tiny tunnels inside the leaf tissue, which are easy to spot on the leaf. This appears as a white or tan squiggly line through the leaf. Sometimes the worms will keep eating until the leaves look like a mosaic. Simply remove the infected leaf.

Caterpillars can show up to feast on your Tulasi. If your leaves are getting munched, take a closer look. Caterpillars are adept at disguising themselves by camouflaging with the plant. Certain kinds come out to feed only at night; yet, the damage they leave behind will be a sure sign of their presence the next morning. The easiest solution is to simply remove the hungry feeders to a far away location. You may need to do some night spotting with a flashlight to catch all of the culprits.

## *Diseases*

Diseases can be caused by fungi, viruses and bacteria. Water logging and improper drainage create bacterial and fungal diseases that cause the roots to rot. Tulasi's leaves will turn yellow and parts of the plant may begin to die. To prevent these diseases from taking hold, always allow for proper soil aeration, and take care not to over water.

Certain viruses can spread to plants through insects. A virus may show up as streaks, spots or curling leaves, and can be difficult to treat. In some cases, a virus may only attack a part of the plant. If this occurs, then carefully remove that section immediately.

High humidity and lack of air circulation can cause fungal mildews to create fuzzy patches on leaves, making them turn brown and die. Other types of fungi may cause healthy leaves to suddenly drop from the plant and an entire branch to wilt. Increasing air circulation, watering as little as possible and dusting your Tulasi with sulphur may stop the spread of fungus. Spraying milk can also be an effective cure for mildews.

Sudden changes in temperature frequently cause disease-like symptoms, such as leaves dropping. Be cautious when growing Tulasi near a window, as hot temperatures in the day and cold temperatures at night can create this kind of shock.

May the information given here be helpful to you in the journey of cultivating your sacred Tulasi plant. Most important is the love and communion you share with Her, as Tulasi Herself will reveal to you what She needs and how to care for Her. In the process, you may find that She is actually the one who has been caring for you, awakening your awareness and nurturing your innate connection with Mother Nature. In the same way, when we cultivate our love and devotion for God, we realise that the Divine is the one truly loving us, helping us grow closer to our true nature.

## The Inner Tulasi ~ Developing Devotion Within

When caring for Tulasi, we can remember that we are nurturing the sweet plant of devotion within our hearts. The sincere desire to love and serve the whole of creation is the soil in which we plant the seeds of pure love. The fertiliser that enhances this desire for selflessness is the discernment we have gained from seeing the gifts in every situation we have encountered. With our lives rooted in patience and humility, we are able to grow fully.

The sun of wisdom (*jnana surya*) is the light that provides ideal conditions for pure love to flourish in our hearts. We can water the plant of devotion with gratitude and loving deeds, while protecting it from the coldness of selfishness and unkindness. Through self-awareness, we can identify 'pests', and prune that which is draining our life energy. By removing 'older leaves', tendencies that hinder growth are released. As a result of mindful care, fragrant flowers of grace emerge. In gratitude, we offer these blossoms as a garland for the Divine.

Amma emphasises awareness as the most important quality for our spiritual development. Always giving us words of encouragement, Amma prays;

> *"May the tree of our life be firmly rooted in the soil of Love. May good deeds be the fruits on that tree, may words of kindness form its flowers and may peace be its fruits. Let us grow and unfold as one family united in Love."*

## Chapter 6

# Cultivation at Amma's Ashram in India

## Amma's Tulasi Garden

In 2003, Amma expressed Her wish to have a large Tulasi garden grown at Her ashram in India. Over time, a grove of coconut trees and an extension of an old parking lot were slowly and lovingly transformed into a lush and vibrant garden filled with Tulasi. A large Tulasi spiral was carved out in the centre of the garden, where all who wished could learn and practice the traditional prayers and circumbulation of the Tulasi plants.

The initial work in the garden was soon flooded by a five-foot wave of saltwater, as the 2004 Asian Tsunami hit the nearby shore of the Arabian Sea, destroying plants and trees, and sadly, the homes of the neighbouring villagers. As homes were being rebuilt by the ashram, the garden regained life, and offered some hope to the devastated area.

## *Tulasi Devi,* the Goddess of Devotion

The Tulasi garden has provided international visitors and ashram residents a chance to participate in an extensive learning process. It has been an opportunity to explore organic farming in the tropics, permaculture, traditional farming techniques of India and the challenge of cultivating during the monsoon season, as well as the ins and outs of growing Tulasi. The fruits of the harvest have been plentiful. An abundance of Tulasi has been provided for offerings to Amma and medicine-making. Over time, and with the addition of flowers, trees, ayurvedic plants and some vegetables, less space was available for the Tulasi.

Amma continued to express Her wish for more and more Tulasi plants to be grown. The garden expanded to new and larger areas a number of times. In 2005, Amma began a much larger project, with the goal of growing 100,000 Tulasi plants.

One of the areas where Amma chose to expand the growing project was eight acres of land on which Amma's ashram had built temporary shelters for hundreds of villagers affected by the Tsunami. This small area of the ocean-side village is called Srayikkad. During the Tsunami, a temple was destroyed in Srayikkad. Amma later said that

*Cultivation at Amma's Ashram in India*

part of Her purpose in having Tulasi plants grown there was to restore the sacred energy of the land. A new temple was built, and along with this, a small group of gardeners have endeavoured to create a living temple of Tulasi Devi.

At the start of the project, approximately twelve families still lived in the shelters. A large group of children from these shelters took the Tulasi garden to be their own. They helped with planting, harvesting, watering and all other aspects of the garden work. With a lot of enthusiasm, very few tools and large area of swampy land, the proj-

ect managed to take root with 5,000 plants. This was quite a surprise, considering the innumerable challenges, which included growing plants in pure sand! The leaf tops and flowers are currently harvested from this garden to weave a daily supply of Tulasi garlands for devotees to offer to Amma. The wood of the branches harvested there is used to create hand-carved prayer beads.

Soon, another area was chosen beside the campus of the ashram's large Ayurvedic Institute and Hospital. This site has been able to cultivate up to 10,000 Tulasi plants at a time. There, international visitors and residents, along with village helpers, work together to cultivate the Tulasi plants.

A unique drying facility was developed in the ashram's Ayurvedic Seaside Building to safely process the Tulasi harvest, in order to provide Tulasi tea for use in India and abroad. Tulasi tincture, Tulasi flower essence, blessed Tulasi leaves (from garlands worn by Amma), healing salves and special tea blends are some of the current medicines being produced from the Tulasi grown in the ashram.

## The Divine Mother's Field

*The follwing story was inspired in one of Amma's Tulasi gardens.*

Come friends, let us go quickly to the fields of Tulasi. Outside the gates of Amma's ashram, just beyond the river, our path is lit by the first rays of the rising sun. The morning sounds of the nearby village can be heard in the distance. We must get to the field just in time for the sun to shine His rays on our Beloved Tulasi. We are rushing to be reunited with Tulasi Devi, the embodiment of the Divine Mother, and we can feel Her awaiting our arrival. As we walk along the river, the cows are just waking, mooing softly, and the birds fill the air with their songs. Our minds and spirits go back to the ancient time of Lord Krishna who roamed in the Tulasi-filled forests of Vrindavan. Our hearts race to greet the field, which is bathed in the soft orange light of dawn.

We walk softly upon the grass, our feet collecting dew, as the gentle, warm breeze blows. The fresh scent of a new day fills us with energy and vitality. We turn onto the cobblestone road that leads us to the field of our Mother Tulasi. We have reached there just in time for the sun's rays to shine through Tulasi's young, light green leaves.

## *Tulasi Devi,* the Goddess of Devotion

The plants that have received the strongest sunlight have turned into different shades of purple. There, in the silence of the dawn, we sit close to Her and gaze at Her with love as She showers Her blessings upon us.

One by one, we file into a circle around one Tulasi plant, which we have planted in a special pot called a matham. We are quiet for a few moments, feeling the stillness. Placing our palms together in prayer, we sing the Tulasi mantras

## Cultivation at Amma's Ashram in India

that have been chanted for ages by those who adore Her.

Bowing with deep reverence to Tulasi, we sit for some time, breathing in the heavenly fragrance that pervades the air. One cannot describe the scent that emits from the Tulasi plants; yet its effect is one of calmness, serenity and peace of mind. Tulasi is known to purify the atmosphere where She grows; and in turn, helps to ward off disease. Any stress dissolves in each breath we take. We are reminded of the importance of slowing down and connecting with Nature, the Source from which we all have come and to which we shall return. We remember Amma's teaching – as we spend time with Tulasi, we are cultivating the awareness of our oneness with all of Nature.

With our hearts open and full of devotion, we begin to sing in unison. In a nearby coconut tree, we see a blue bird who is joining us in song. Forgetting ourselves, we merge into the sweet melodies of songs of love to the Divine Mother. Tulasi Devi has come; and She is calling us to share our sorrows, joys and our hearts with Her. We bow down deeply once more to Tulasi Devi and She showers us with Her blessings of love and devotion.

## *Tulasi Devi,* the Goddess of Devotion

Upon rising from the earth, we look out into the beautiful field of the Divine Mother. She is dancing in the warm wind, and the gentle breezes are caressing Her. Like little children, we scatter and run out into the field to jump, play or lay in the arms of our Mother. The very soil that Tulasi grows from is known to be sacred. Lying under Her branches, cradled in Her lap, one feels this to be true. Peering into the blue sky, we feel expansive and connected with all of Creation.

The soil here is a combination of sand and red mud, with composted cow manure. Tulasi loves the sun and humidity, and She thrives here in the warm, moist air. Amma has told us that the Tulasi that grows in Kerala is very potent as the temperature, sunlight and other conditions, create the optimal atmosphere for Her to grow.

Although the tropical weather provides many months of strong sunlight, the monsoon rains can come and go for up to six months. At times, the field is nearly flooded. We have planted Tulasi in raised beds, as She cannot survive long if Her roots are drowned in water. During the monsoon, many Tulasi plants struggle to survive. However, this morning the plants are in full bloom. Morning is a good time to harvest since the energy of the plant is moving upwards. There is a special mantra that we chant before beginning to harvest.

*Tulasi amrita-janmasi*
*Sada tvam Kesava-priya*
*Kesavartham cinomi tvam*
*Varada bhava shobane*

Oh Tulasi, You are born from nectar,
You are eternally dear to Lord Keshava,
It is for Lord Keshava that we collect your leaves,
Oh beautiful Tulasi,
please grant us the blessing of serving the Lord.

Harvesting Tulasi's leaves, flowers and seeds is a very special task. It is believed that when a Tulasi branch is broken unnecessarily, Lord Krishna feels the pain as his own. We feel honoured and privileged to be able to touch the Tulasi, and do so with our utmost care and attention.

Sitting beside Her, we pray with all of our hearts to forgive us if we make any mistakes while harvesting Her leaves. We remember what Amma has told us, that the medicine we make for others should be created with prayer and remembrance of God. As this Tulasi will be used to make garlands that will be offered to Amma, love overflows from our hearts. We imagine Amma wearing these garlands that represent the love of the Earth Herself. Each Tulasi leaf trembles with joy and gratitude for the opportunity to serve to the Divine. One can almost hear them singing, "Choose me. Take me. Let us all reunite with the One who created us." We giggle, knowing that She is already one with the Divine Mother, that they are never separate from each other. This is the sweetness of devotion that Tulasi helps to cultivate within us.

As we harvest, we watch the tiny bees that fit right inside of the Tulasi flowers to receive their daily food from Her. These are very special bees that only take the nectar from medicinal herbs. Below the flowering stalk, we can harvest down two or three nodes. Within a few days, there will be two stalks growing instead of one. This is the magic of Tulasi. By sharing Her leaves, She actually grows larger, and is able to offer more of Herself to the world. She teaches us that if we focus on giving, instead of taking from the world, we will gain so much more in life.

The sun has now risen high in the sky, and the Tulasi plants are beginning to wilt in the heat. This is an indication that we should stop harvesting. We join back together in the shade of the coconut trees to see how the harvest went for the morning. The tiny bees follow us to where we sit. They land on us from time to time, quietly kissing our hands that have been stained deep purple by the Tulasi.

After harvesting, we turn our attention to nourishing the plants. We first add compost to help enrich the soil. We then spend some time mulching around the Tulasi plants. Mulch occurs naturally in all forests, and we try to mimic the litter layer of a forest floor. This litter layer is a nutrient-rich bed of decaying leaves, twigs and branches. The nutrients from the decaying matter break down over time and the plants absorb these nutrients. We never leave the soil bare. If it becomes bare, water is more likely to erode the soil and expose the tender roots of the plants. Bare soil can also dry out, losing some of its fertility.

We are humbly trying to create Vrindavan here in this field of Tulasi, as this is Amma's wish. Vrindavan was a forest where all animals, plants and humans lived peacefully side by side under the divine guidance of Lord Krishna. Krishna knew the hearts of all beings there. It was a place of great bio-diversity, where a weed was not seen as a weed but as a plant that also was yearning to have the sight and touch of the Lord.

## *Tulasi Devi,* the Goddess of Devotion

Let us pray that we are able to fulfil Amma's wish to create this forest of love once again. May all beings learn to live together again in harmony, and experience their connection with Nature as that of a child with her mother.

# Chapter 7

# Insights and Experiences

## The Wealth of Selflessness

Swami Premananda was one of the first young men to come live with Amma in 1979. Under Amma's guidance, he now runs an ashram on Reunion Island, off the coast of Africa. He has always had a great love of plants, especially Tulasi. When first establishing the ashram there, Amma had told him to purchase land in a sparse area of the Island. She then asked him to grow a beautiful garden in the otherwise barren area, saying, "Anybody can grow a garden where it is fertile, but to grow a garden in a desert, one needs real love."

During one of Amma's first visits to Reunion, a very poor man came to see Her. He was carrying a basket of young Krishna Tulasi saplings. He handed the basket to Amma, asking Her to bless the baby plants. He told Amma that he was a very poor man and that he had nothing else to offer, yet he wished to sell these Tulasi plants to raise money for Amma's orphanage. Amma joyfully exclaimed, "How can you be a poor man? A poor person cannot give, but you are giving. Therefore, you are a rich man! There are many rich people who cannot give. They are the truly poor ones."

Amma lovingly held the basket of Tulasi plants on top of Her head and began to chant sweetly, "Krishna, Krishna!" As she chanted, Her devotion sent Her into a deep state of bliss. Witnessing this touching scene, Swami Premananda was so moved that he, himself, purchased all of the Tulasi plants in the basket. He planted the sacred young plants in the ashram garden. They soon grew to be large and beautiful, creating a heavenly garden lush with life and sanctity.

Once, Swami Premananda recalled a verse from the scriptures stating that if one lovingly gazes at Tulasi with devotion in the early morning hours, one will enjoy perfect eyesight for the rest of his life. Knowing that the modern mind needs scientific facts in order to prove these types of scriptural statements, he resolved to look into this further.

After a long search, he discovered research confirming that Tulasi releases a special vapour, along with ozone, during the early morning stages of photosynthesis. He felt that when one gazes with devotion, the eyes may become moist or filled with tears. He recalled the shining twinkle of Amma's eyes that always seems to be brimming with tears of love. He thought, "What else but this moisture of devotion, could make the eyes best able to absorb the benefit of the vapours?"

Swami Premananda shared another interesting story about a famous Tulasi plant in Bangalore, India. The Tulasi was reported to be five metres tall and had lived for 20 years. The house in which the extraordinary Tulasi grows belongs to a woman who has devoutly worshipped Tulasi Devi since she was a young girl. She faithfully practices the traditional ritual of worshipping Tulasi each morning with her heart filled with love. People from all over India visit the famous Tulasi. They believe that it is due to the woman's sincere devotion that the Tulasi has thrived for so many years.

## The Living Goddess

For the past several years, India has been suffering a continuing epidemic of suicide amongst its farmers. One study recently showed farmers in some regions committing suicide at a rate of one person every eight hours! Many farmers are being encouraged by aggressive economic forces to switch from growing traditional food crops to a monoculture of cash cropping. To do this, they often take large loans. Simultaneously, there are increasing incidences of crop failures due to droughts, depleted soil and the failure of chemical pesticides. Feeling desperate with land that is producing no yield, mountains of debt and no hope of providing for their families, these farmers take their lives by drinking pesticides.

Amma's compassion for the tragic plight of these farmers inspired Her to do everything possible to help. Amongst the many projects initiated by Amma's ashram, the Mata Amritanandamayi Math (MAM), are permanent scholarships to 100,000 children of farmers living below the poverty line. Many of the beneficiaries are children who have lost one or both parents to suicide. Awareness campaigns, including programmes aimed at instilling and strengthening universal values in youth are underway. Furthermore, special advanced-education camps and symposiums on environmental preservation are being conducted. MAM is also providing free vocational training for 5,000 self-help groups of women from impoverished agricultural families.

Recently, some of these poor families visited Amma's main ashram in southern India. As they experienced daily life at the ashram, they felt very much at home. In fact, they were amazed to see a large swing hanging from the trees beside Amma's room, which was very much like the ones they played with during their childhood. The women quite boldly played on the swing, standing up on it and swinging, ready to pluck the leaves from the highest branches in their mouths just as they did as children. "We feel we are in our mother's house," was their happy refrain.

Early in the morning, as they were preparing to leave, some of them went to the garden by Amma's room and collected soil from beneath the swing to take to their homes. Doing so, they said, "If we visit God's place of worship, we should bring its remembrance with us but we do not have sufficient money to bring back anything. Hence, we are taking this soil, which has been touched by Amma's Divine Feet. We will plant Tulasi in this sacred soil, in remembrance of Amma's presence. Amma is in our hearts. Until now, we have seen God only in deities made of stone, but here we have seen the Living God. In remembrance of the Living Goddess, we are taking this sacred soil for planting Tulasi Devi in our homes. We are going to plant a Living Goddess!"

The innocent faith with which they shared these words moved many to tears. For these simple villagers who have suffered such tragic losses, Tulasi is not just a symbol. She is the Divine Mother incarnate. Knowing the hope and strength that Tulasi brings into their lives and homes, they plant Her as the embodiment of compassion and a tangible form of ever-new life.

## Chapter 8

# Legends of Tulasi Devi

*"Religion teaches us to worship God within Nature. Through the stories of Sri Krishna's life, the Tulasi plant and the cow have become very dear to the people of India, who lovingly protect and look after them. In times past, there would be a pond and a small grove of trees adjoining every house in India. Each home had a Tulasi plant growing in the front yard. Part of the daily routine in those days was to water the Tulasi plant every morning, bowing down with reverence and devotion in front of it, worshipping it as an embodiment of the Goddess.*

*"In the old days, there was no specific need for environmental preservation because protecting Nature was part of worshipping God and life itself. More than remembering 'God', the people used to love and serve Nature and society. They saw the Creator through the creation. They loved, worshipped and protected Nature as the visible form of God." – Amma*

## *Tulasi Devi,* the Goddess of Devotion

There are numerous stories throughout the scriptures of India describing the glories and virtues of Tulasi Devi and how She came into being as a sacred plant. Tulasi Devi is worshipped as the very embodiment of pure devotion to God. Amma says that Tulasi is the flower of self-sacrifice. It is said that worshipping the embodiment of devotion in the form of this humble plant awakens pure love, devotion and humility within us.

Tulasi is most closely associated with Lord Krishna, who is beautifully described in the following quote, "The Supreme Lord, the embodiment of Truth, Consciousness and Joy is known as Krishna, or Govinda. He has no beginning, is the origin of everything, and the cause of all causes."
– Brahma Samhita 5

Sri Krishna is one of the incarnations of Lord Vishnu, God in the aspect of the sustainer of the universe. Considered the most beloved of Lord Vishnu, as His purest and most exalted devotee, Tulasi is honoured as an incarnation of the Goddess of Life. It is said that Lord Vishnu, for the upliftment of all beings, created Tulasi from the cosmic, milky ocean that produced the nectar of immortality.

She is worshipped with a well-known chant that proclaims:

*Yadmule sarvatirthani*
*Yadagre sarva devataam*
*Yadmadhye sarva vedaascha*
*Tulasi taam namaamyaham.*

I bow to Tulasi,
upon whose roots reside all the sacred rivers;
In whose branches and leaves reside all the Gods,
And whose crown is the Vedas.

Worshippers of Lord Vishnu (*Vaishnavites*), believe Tulasi to be an embodiment of Vrinda Devi, the Goddess of all plants and trees. Vrinda Devi is also known as the manifesting power behind the divine play of God or Lila-shakti. She resides in the celestial realm of Lord Krishna, known as Goloka. Vrindavan is the manifestation of Goloka on Earth, and was the childhood abode of Lord Krishna. Everything that happens in Vrindavan is said to occur by the will of Vrinda Devi. To please the Lord, She decides how the wind blows, where it rains, and which flowers will blossom. Vrinda Devi manifested ages before the decent of Lord Krishna on earth, and performed

## *Tulasi Devi,* the Goddess of Devotion

many intense spiritual practices. The place where She undertook these austerities was sanctified and named Vrindavan.

One legend from the Brahma Vaivraata Purana tells that Goddess Lakshmi took birth on earth in order to enact a divine play and to help the Gods overtake a powerful demon. She was born on the full moon day in the month of Kartika, as the extraordinarily beautiful daughter of King Dharmadhwaja. Her beauty and divine qualities inspired the sages to name Her Tulasi, or 'The Incomparable One'.

From birth itself, She performed intense austerities to attain Her beloved Lord Krishna as Her husband. However, She was bound to wed Shankhacuda, who was once a close devotee of Lord Krishna, but had been cursed to become a demon on earth. Shankhacuda had also performed austerities to gain the saintly Tulasi as his wife. To fulfil this destiny, Tulasi was married to him. Shankhacuda drew so much strength from the purity and chastity of Tulasi that he was invincible in battle. Consequently, he became egotistical and began to fight with the peaceful demigods (*devas*).

The devas went to Lord Vishnu, pleading for His help. Lord Vishnu promised to help them

## Legends of Tulasi Devi

restore harmony once again. The Lord knew that, through this, He would also liberate Shankhacuda from the delusion of his demon form, and fulfil the true yearning of Tulasi. Lord Vishnu assumed the form of Tulasi's demon husband and went to visit Her. When She received Him, thinking Him to be Shankhacuda, Tulasi's chastity was momentarily broken. Taking advantage of this, the devas overtook Shankhacuda. At that moment, Shankhacuda was freed from the curse and reunited with his Lord.

When Tulasi came to know what had happened, She accused Lord Vishnu of acting in a stone-hearted manner and declared that He should become a stone. Honouring Her purity and devotion, the Lord accepted Her words wholeheartedly. He then promised to appear on earth as a Shaligrama shila. The Shaligrama shilas are sacred stones that appear only in the Gandaki River that flows between the Dhaulagiri and Annapurna mountain ranges of the Himalayas.

He gave Tulasi the benediction that She would eternally reside with Him as His beloved in the spiritual realm. He then declared, that for the benefit of creation, Tulasi would assume the form

## *Tulasi Devi*, the Goddess of Devotion

of a sacred plant, which would bless all beings with pure devotion.

Lord Vishnu told Tulasi, "The leaves of this plant will be considered the most sacred in all the three worlds and will be used in all worship ceremonies (pujas) done to me. All holy rivers will reside at the foot of the Tulasi plant, and all places where You are cultivated will become pure and holy. All the Gods will remain at Your holy feet awaiting the falling of a single leaf. I will get more joy from the offering of a single Tulasi leaf than from offerings of countless gems and holy waters (87)."

It is said that Tulasi's body, itself, then became the Gandaki River and Her beautiful hair became the sacred Tulasi plants. Even to this day, devotees pilgrimage to the Gandaki River to collect the sacred Shaligrama shila stones and worship them with holy Tulasi leaves.

Such stories from the Puranas always hold a deeper significance. As Tulasi lived a pure and righteous life of deep devotion and longing for God, the Lord blessed Her by removing Her attachment, obstacles and worldly bondage. Her surrender and acceptance made Her an instrument to serve the greater good of all, and in the end, Her pure prayers were fulfilled by the Lord.

Sometimes, as in this legend, we may also misunderstand the workings of the Divine or even blame God. Yet, the ever-compassionate Lord forgives us and constantly turns life's challenges into blessings. The Lord sanctified Tulasi so that, through Her self-sacrifice, She would become an offering to the whole of creation. Thus, She became His own beloved, eternally inseparable from Him.

The word *Tulasi* is derived from the word *thula*, which translates as 'to lift up'. Tulasi is said to lift us all up to the Lord's side. Another translation is 'a balance for the measurement of weights'. *Thula saadhrusyam* means 'resembling that of the balance in equipoise', and points to the state of even-mindedness. One well-known legend tells of a time when Lord Krishna was being weighed against an immense amount of gold; yet, the scales would not balance. Then, when the Lord's consort, Rukmini, lovingly placed a single Tulasi leaf on the scale, it became balanced. In this way, Tulasi revealed how even the smallest object, when offered with love and devotion, means more to the Lord than all the wealth in the world.

## *Tulasi Devi*, the Goddess of Devotion

Another Tulasi legend is connected to the birth of Bhu Devi. The Goddess Maha Lakshmi was born on earth in a beautiful garden of Tulasi. The enlightened sage, Markandeya, found the Goddess as a lovely, tiny baby girl under a Tulasi plant. Naming Her Bhu Devi, meaning 'of the earth', he raised Her as his own daughter. She grew to be a beautiful maiden. One day, Lord Vishnu came to earth and disguised Himself as an old man seeking the hand of Bhu Devi in marriage. Although at first reluctant, it was at last revealed to Markandeya that the old man to whom he was giving his daughter in marriage was none other than the Lord. After wedding Bhu Devi, Lord Vishnu promised to remain there in that holy Tulasi garden for all time. A famous temple, Thiruvinnagaram, considered one of the celebrated 108 abodes of Lord Vishnu, still exists in that sacred place.

A similar story appears in the life of Andal, a famous Tamil woman saint and divine poetess. There was once a humble Brahmin, named Vishnucitta, living near Madurai, who daily picked flowers for the worship of the Lord. One day he discovered an enchanting baby girl lying under a sacred Tulasi plant in his flower garden. Believ-

*Legends of Tulasi Devi*

ing God's grace gave him this baby, he named her Godai, meaning the 'gift of Mother Earth'. Young Godai manifested unusually intense devotion for the Lord. She would always adorn herself with the flower garlands that had been prepared for the Lord, imagining herself to be His bride. Vishnuchitta could not understand the mysterious ways of His daughter, until one night he had a powerful dream in which the Lord revealed His pleasure with the innocent devotion of Godai. He told Vishnucitta that He would only accept the garlands that had first been worn by Godai. Vishnucitta realised that his daughter was someone whose love of God was so intense and pure that the Lord Himself wished to share in her presence. From this day on, she became known as Andal, the girl who ruled over the Lord.

As she grew up, she composed poems of such heart-stirring devotion that they are still loved and read to this day. At the age of fifteen, during a ceremony in which she was being married to her beloved deity, Lord Ranganath, she merged into a blaze of light in the inner shrine of the temple. Today, the blessed Tulasi garden in which Andal was found is preserved in Srivilliputtur, along with a temple dedicated to this divine saint.

## *Tulasi Devi,* the Goddess of Devotion

Tulasi is revered as a potent means of attaining pure devotion (bhakti). One story in the Srimad Bhagavatam tells of Tulasi's power to awaken bhakti in our hearts. The four Kumaras were the sons of Lord Brahma, who is the formless aspect of God. Since their spiritual path was that of wisdom and knowledge, they were not inclined in any way towards bhakti. "When the breeze, carrying the aroma of Tulasi leaves and saffron from the holy feet of the lotus-eyed Lord Krishna entered through the nostrils, into the hearts of those sages (the Kumaras), they experienced a change in both body and mind, even though they were attached to the impersonal Brahman understanding." (Canto 3, Chapter 15, Srimad Bhagavatam.) Hence, by simply smelling the fragrance of Tulasi, the four Kumaras were transformed, and became pure devotees of Lord Krishna.

There is a beautiful story from the Sri Garga Samathi about how saintly Radha, the beloved of Krishna, worshipped Tulasi. As the tale goes, Radha brought the sacred Tulasi plant to the middle of a forest, and with deep devotion, humbly followed a vow of worshipping Her for seven months. After completing the vow, Radha attained a vision of the lovely four-armed Tulasi

Goddess descending from the sky to embrace Her. Radha asked Tulasi Devi to grant Her supreme and unalloyed devotion for the lotus feet of Lord Krishna. Tulasi graciously fulfilled Radha's wish. This story demonstrates the great level of faith that is placed in Tulasi, who is capable of granting absolute devotion to Radha, who is considered an embodiment of selfless love for the Lord.

## Praise from the Scriptures

Innumerable verses from the scriptures praise the endless virtues of Tulasi. Following are some verses that illustrate deep reverence for Her powers of pure love and healing.

"Just by looking at Tulasi, all one's sins are removed. Just by touching Her, one's body becomes pure. By praying to Her, all diseases are removed. If one waters Her or makes Her wet, the fear of Yamaraja (death personified) is destroyed. Just by planting or transplanting, one achieves nearness to the Supreme. If someone offers Tulasi at the lotus feet of Lord Sri Krishna, Tulasi awards liberation and devotion to that individual.

Therefore, I pay my humble obeisance to such a wonderful Tulasi Devi."

– Hari Bhakti Vilasa, 9/104,
from Skanda Purana, 3000 BC

"Tulasi is auspicious in all respects. Simply by seeing, simply by touching, simply by remembering, simply by praying to, simply by bowing before, simply by hearing about, or simply by sowing the tree, there is always auspiciousness. Anyone who comes in touch with the Tulasi tree in the above-mentioned ways lives eternally in the Vaikuntha (spiritual world)."

– Bhakti Rasamrita Sindhu from the Skanda Purana

"Wherever the aroma of Tulasi is carried by the wind, it purifies the atmosphere and frees all animals from their baser tendencies."

– Padmapurana, Uttarakhanda

"Every home with a Tulasi plant is a place of pilgrimage, and no diseases, or messengers of Yama (the God of Death), can enter it."

– Skandapurana 2, 4, 8, 13 Padmapurana, Uttarakhanda

## Amma's Story of the Tulasi and Lotus

"One full-moon night during the spring season, Lord Krishna came to dance with the gopis. The gopis were the beloved ones of Lord Sri Krishna. Surrounded by the gopis, robed in yellow silk, with a peacock feather tucked into His curly hair and a garland of Tulasi leaves around His neck, holding a Lotus in His hand, Krishna shined like the full moon amidst the stars. They danced until dawn. Finally, the exhausted gopis sat down in a circle around Sri Krishna.

"One gopi asked, 'Lord, even though there are so many beautiful and fragrant flowers in Vrindavan, Dear Lord, why do you like the Tulasi and Lotus so much?' Krishna replied, 'These are not ordinary flowers. They are the flowers of self-sacrifice.' The gopi asked, 'Why are they called the flowers of self-sacrifice?' Krishna replied by telling them the story behind the Tulasi and Lotus.

*"Once a little dirt clod and a dry leaf were playing hide and seek. As they were playing, they saw a jasmine flower tumbling toward them in the wind. They asked the jasmine, 'Where are you going?' 'Didn't you know?' said the jasmine flower, 'The Lord is going to come this way. If one lies in*

*His path and touches His feet, it is enough to gain liberation. That is what I am going to do.' Without even waiting a second, the jasmine tumbled off in the wind.*

"*The little dirt clod and the dry leaf talked to themselves, 'Why don't we also go and wait on the path? Who knows if we will get an opportunity like this again?' So they went and saved themselves a spot on the Lord's path. Soon, a gopi came along and swept away the dry leaf saying, 'I just swept this area and, now look, a dry leaf has appeared again.' Another gopi then kicked away the dirt clod saying, 'I just finished spreading fresh sand over this path. Where did this dirt clod come from?'*

"*Poor things. With whom can the little dirt clod and dry leaf share their sorrows? The Lord is the only one they can call their own, but if this is what they experience when they try and get only a tiny glimpse of the Lord, then who can they turn to for help?*

"*The dirt clod said, 'No one likes us. Wherever we go, they see us as dirty and useless. What is the point in living when we are just a burden to Mother Earth? It is better to pray to be reborn as a flower or grain of sand on the Lord's path and put an end to this life.' But the dry leaf said back,*

'It is due to our karma that we received this useless birth. Even still, we have been lucky enough to hear about Lord Krishna. So it is better that we make use of this life that God has given us, and be of some use to someone before dying. At least then we can expect a better birth next time.'

"As they brooded over their sorrows, noon came and the sun's light cast down like fire. But for those who are burning in the fire of sorrow, the external sunlight does not feel hot at all. Suddenly, they heard the sound of someone crying. When they looked around, they saw a black seed. The dirt clod asked, 'Who are you? Why are you crying?'

"'I am a Lotus seed and I am about to die due to the sunlight. If there were only someone who could push me into the pond, then I would be saved.' The dirt clod replied, 'If I come in contact with water, then I will dissolve into nothingness, but that is okay because at least you will be saved. Let me be of that much use to the world.' Saying so, the little dirt clod took the seed and rolled into the pond.

"After his inseparable friend left, the dry leaf's sorrow doubled. Suddenly, he heard a soft cry. He could not see anyone, but as the cries continued, he looked more carefully and saw a seed that was even smaller than a mustard seed. 'Why are you *crying,' the leaf asked? The seed replied, 'I am a Tulasi seed. I am about to die in the heat of the sun. I am crying and praying to God to give me some shade.' 'Oh, let me be of some use to you,' said the dry leaf. And it covered the tiny Tulasi seed. The leaf constantly protected the seed in the sun, wind, snow and rain and was finally powdered into nothing.*

"Lord Krishna concluded the story to the gopis: 'My dear ones, when I see the Tulasi and Lotus, I remember the sacrifice of the dirt clod and dry leaf. It is the unknown sacrifice of those whom the world sees as useless and insignificant that gives fragrance to the flowers. This is the beauty of the earth. We all have the feeling of I and mine like the dirt clod and dry leaf. They are considered impure and are unwanted wherever they go. It is because of this ego and attachment that we feel rejected. The feeling of I and mine is the reason why we never experience the presence of God. When we are able to destroy this ego and attachment for the sake of removing another's sorrow, then we become the beloved of God. We will never be able to be separate from God.

"The dirt clod is a hard and firm mass of vasanas, or negative tendencies, devoid of the moisture of kindness and consideration. When it comes into contact with the water of love and devotion, it dissolves into nothingness. Only then, will the flowers of selflessness blossom. In the same way, the dry leaf represents the fallen leaves of the past. When this leaf disintegrates into nothing, it becomes the fertiliser for the ripe fruits of the present moment."

The Tulasi seed and the Lotus seed symbolise the seeds of spiritual awakening within us. As Amma describes, when we cultivate selflessness and dissolve our negativities, these seeds can take root. The sacred Tulasi plant, adored as the most beloved of the Lord, and the fully-blossomed Lotus are beautiful symbols of an intimate connection to the Divine that we can all experience. Practising self-sacrifice, humility and living in the present moment are some of the ways that Amma teaches us to grow and experience that we are truly one with God.

# Chapter 9

# Traditional Worship and Rituals

*"The relationship between humanity and Nature is like the relationship between Pindanada (the Microcosm) and Brahmanada (the Macrocosm). Our great ancestors understood this. That is why they gave so much importance to Nature worship in religious practices. The idea behind all religious practices was to closely associate human beings with Nature. By establishing a loving relationship between humanity and Nature, they ensured both the balance of Nature and the progress of the human race... [The Ancients] knew that trees, plants and animals were absolutely necessary for the benefit and good of humans. They foresaw that humanity, in its selfish moments, would forget Nature and cease to have any concern for Her. They also knew that future generations would suffer due to humanity's disassociation from Nature. Therefore, they linked each religious rite with Nature. Thus, through religious principles, they*

*could succeed in developing an emotional bond between humanity and Nature. The Ancients loved and worshipped trees and plants such as the Tulasi, banyan tree, and Bilva, not because the trees bore fruit and helped them to make a profit, but because the Ancients knew that they, themselves, in truth, were one with all of Nature."*
— *Amma*

Amma says that the tradition of worshipping Tulasi as the Goddess is a powerful practice that will help to re-establish the harmony between humanity and Nature. The Tulasi *puja* (worship ceremony) is symbolic of worshipping all of Mother Nature. Amma recommends that we light a lamp in front of Tulasi Devi early in the morning and walk around Her several times. The principle behind this worship is that by beholding the divinity in these plants, we will recognise and honour the Divine in all aspects of creation. As we develop our love and reverence for Mother Nature, our every action will be guided by the awareness of protecting and caring for Her.

Out of respect for Her sanctity, Tulasi is traditionally planted at the entrance of the home or temple in a raised structure called a Tulasi *matham*. The Tulasi *matham* often has spiritual

## *Tulasi Devi,* the Goddess of Devotion

symbols and/or deities carved on all four of its sides, and many contain an alcove for a small oil lamp. Some households may grow many Tulasi plants together to form a tiny sacred Tulasi forest,

called a Tulasi *vana* or Tulasi *Vrindavan.* It is usually the woman of the household who performs the worship to Tulasi, invoking the Mother Goddess to grant devotion, healing, purity, protection

## Traditional Worship and Rituals

and prosperity to the household. The worship ritual includes the lighting of a ghee lamp, offering of water, chanting and singing, circumambulating Tulasi and prostrating before Her.

Tulasi is so respected that prayer beads are carved from Her woody stems and worn in necklaces or malas of 108 beads. The prayer beads are used to practice chanting mantras (*japa*) and to provide protection, healing and spiritual energy.

One of the most precious traditions of worshipping Tulasi is the ceremonial marriage of the Tulasi plant to Lord Vishnu, called the Tulasi *vivaha* or Tulasi *kalyanam*. The Lord is represented as the sacred stone (*Shaligrama shila*) or as the form of Lord Krishna. The Tulasi plant and pot are beautifully decorated with a skirt, jewels and garlands. Ancient mantras are chanted as threads are tied, symbolising their union. Garlands are exchanged and offerings of milk and flowers are given, with all the due reverence and sweetness of a true marriage. This sacred ceremony of the divine couple takes place on the eleventh day of the waxing moon in the month of *Kartika*, which falls some time in October according to the lunar calendar. The ceremony usually continues for five days, concluding on the day of the full moon, and marks the auspicious beginning of the Hindus' annual marriage season.

*"Everything is pervaded by Consciousness. It is that consciousness which sustains the world and all of the creatures in it. To worship everything, seeing God in all, that is what religion advises. Such an attitude teaches us to love Nature."*

*– Amma*

Tulasi is worshipped in the early morning after bathing, with the chanting of the following mantras. The mantras can be sung or chanted in any tune that one prefers. A lamp is traditionally lit. One bows before Tulasi Devi and chants the opening prayer, *Tulasi Pranamma Mantra*. Then, one offers water and circumambulates Tulasi three or four times while chanting the *Tulasi Pradakshina Mantra*.

The *Vaishnavites* worship the Tulasi with the above mantras and also include a *Tulasi Arati*. Camphor is lit in a lamp and waved before Tulasi with the ringing of bells, as a special chant is sung, symbolising the offering of oneself to the Divine. The *Vaishnavites* include worship of Tulasi in their temples, and devotees sing and dance around the Tulasi, worshipping Her with great love. Lord Krishna is always seen wearing a garland of Tulasi

## Tulasi Pranama Mantra

*Vrindayai Tulasi devyai*
*Priyayai keshavasya cha*
*Vishnu bhakti prade devi*
*Satya vatyai namo namah*

*I offer my prayers to Tulasi Devi*
*Who is very dear to Lord Krishna*
*O Goddess, you bestow devotion*
*and possess the highest truth.*


## Tulasi Pradakshina Mantra

*Yani kani cha papani*
*Brahma hatyadikani cha*
*Tani tani pranasyanti*
*Pradakshina pade pade*

*By circumambulating Tulasi Devi*
*All sins committed*
*are destroyed at every step.*

## *Tulasi Devi*, the Goddess of Devotion

around his neck, and Tulasi is always included amongst the sacred offerings.

As Tulasi is highly medicinal, at least one or more leaves can be eaten daily to receive powerful benefits for physical and spiritual well-being. The Tulasi leaf can be eaten fresh or kept in a glass of water placed on an altar or in the sunlight. Adding Tulasi leaves to holy water, or *tirtha*, is an ancient practice followed to this day in temples and homes.

Tulasi is among the eight objects of worship in the ritual of the consecration of the container of holy water called the *kalasa*. This holy water is offered to God during worship, and consumed afterwards as *prasad*. *Prasad* refers to all offerings to the Divine that return to the worshipper with God's blessings. Drinking holy water is said to spiritually uplift us and purify our bodies of disease. Many believe that both the offering and the *prasad* are incomplete without the presence of Tulasi leaves.

Tulasi flowers (*manjaris*) and leaves are traditionally gathered and offered to God. When using leaves for worship, pick only as many as are needed. Amma has said, *"When the realisation dawns within us that everything is pervaded by one and the same consciousness, compassion will arise, and we will sincerely wish to help and protect all. In that state, we won't even feel like picking a leaf unnecessarily."*

The following rare and beautifully in-depth puja expresses a profound devotion for Tulasi as the Divine Mother of the Universe.

## Tulasi Puja

śrī mahā-deva uvāca
The Blessed Great Lord spoke:

**dhyāyec ca tulasīṁ devīṁ śyāmāṁ kamala-locanām
prasanna-padma-kalhāra-varābhaya-caturbhujām**

One should meditate on Tulasi Devi, who has a dark complexion, lotus-eyes, and four beneficent arms, holding the lotus, water lily, and the two gestures of granting boons and giving fearlessness.

**kirīṭa-hāra-keyūra-kuṁḍalādi-vibhūṣitām
dhavalāṁśuka-saṁyuktāṁ padmāsana-niṣeduṣīm**

One should meditate on Tulasi Devi, who is decorated with a crown, garland, bracelets, and earrings; who wears a white garment, and is seated in the lotus posture.

**devi trailokya-janani sarva-lokaika-pāvani
āgaccha bhagavatyatra prasīda tulasi
 drutam**

Oh Devi! Mother of the three worlds, who purifies all worlds, Goddess Tulasi, come!

**sarva-deva-maye devi sarvadā viṣṇu-
 vallabhe
ratna-svarṇa-mayaṁ divyaṁ gṛhāṇāsanam
 avyaye**

Oh Devi! Constant beloved of Visnu, embodiment of all Gods, accept this imperishable, divine seat, made of diamonds and gold.

**sarva-deva-mayākāre sarva-deva-namo 'stute
pādyaṁ gṛhāṇa deveśi tulasi tvaṁ prasīda
 me**

Tulasi! Ruler of all Gods, whose form is of all Gods, may all Gods give salutations to You! May you please bless me, and accept this water for Your feet.

**sarva-deva-mayākāre sarvāgama-niśobhite
idam arghyaṁ gṛhāṇa tvaṁ devi
 daityāntaka-priye**

## Traditional Worship and Rituals

Devi! Thou whose form is of all Gods, who shines with all of the Vedas, and who are the beloved of Lord Visnu, the destroyer of all demons, may You accept this water for Your hands.

**sarva-lokasya rakṣārthaṁ sadā saṁnidhi-kāriṇi**
**gṛhāṇa tulasi prītyā idam ācamanīyakam**

Oh Tulasi! Thou who are always present to protect the entire world, please accept this water for sipping.

**gaṁgādibhyo nadībhyaśca samānītam idaṁ jalam**
**snānārthaṁ tulasi svacchaṁ prītyā tat pratigṛtdyatām**

Oh Tulasi! Please accept for Your bathing this clear water, which is collected from rivers such as the Ganges.

**kṣīroda-mathanodbhūte candra-lakṣmī-sahodare**
**gṛtdyatāṁ paridhānārtham idaṁ kṣaumāṁbaraṁ śubhe**

Oh Auspicious One! Thou who manifested from the churning of the ocean of milk, and who are the sister of both the Moon and Laksmi, please accept this silk garment for wearing.

## *Tulasi Devi,* the Goddess of Devotion

śrī-gaṁdhaṁ kuṁkumaṁ divyaṁ
 karpūrāgaru-saṁyutam
kalpitaṁ te mahā-devi prītyarthaṁ
 pratigṛtdyatām

Oh Great Devi! Please accept this divine kumkum, along with incense, fragrance, camphor and aloe, composed for Your pleasure.

nīlotpalaṁ tu kalhāra-mālatyādīni śobhane
padmādi-gaṁdhavaṁtīni puṣpāṇi
 pratigṛtdyatām

Oh Beautiful One! Please accept these flowers, fragrant like the lotus, the blue lotus, water-lily, and jasmine.

dhūpaṁ gṛhāṇa deveśi mano-hāri
 sa-guggalam
ājya-misraṁ tu tulasi bhaktābhiṣṭa-
 pradāyini

Oh Beautiful One! Ruler of the Gods, Tulasi! Please accept this incense mixed with 'guggala' (tree sap) and ghee, Thou who bless devotees with their desires.

ajñāna-timirāṁdhasya jñāna-dīpa-pradāyinī
tvayā tu tulasi prītā dīpo 'yaṁ
 pratigṛtdyatām

## Traditional Worship and Rituals

Tulasi! Thou who give the lamp of Knowledge that dispels the darkness of Ignorance, please accept this lamp.

**namaste jagatāṁ nāthe prāṇināṁ priya-darśane
yathā-śakti mayā dattaṁ naivedyaṁ pratigṛtdyatām**

Salutations to You, Ruler of the universe! Thou who are of pleasing form to all creatures, please accept this *naivedyam* (food offering) which is offered by me according to my own ability.

**namo bhagavate śreṣṭhe nārāyana-jagan-maye
tulasi tvarayā devi pānīyaṁ pratigṛtdyatām**

Oh Tulasi Devi! Salutations to You, Goddess, who are most great, who exist as both the Lord Visnu and as the universe. Quickly, please accept this water for drinking.

**amṛte mṛta-saṁbhūte tulasyamṛta-rūpiṇi
karpūrādi-samāyuktaṁ tāṁbūlaṁ pratigṛtdyatām**

Oh Tulasi! Thou whose nature is immortal, who is immortal, yet manifest from the perishable, please accept this betel-nut chew, along with an offering of camphor.

dakṣiṇā dakṣiṇa-kare tvad-bhaktānāṁ
   priyaṁ-kari
karomi te sadā bhaktyā viṣṇu-kānte
   pradakṣiṇām

Oh Thou who are pleasing to devotees, I offer a *daksina* (money offering) with my right hand to You, with constant devotion. Oh beloved of Lord Visnu, I perform circumambulation to You.

namo namo jagad-dhatryai jagad-ādyai
   namo namaḥ
namo namo jagad-bhūtyai namaste
   parameśvari

Salutations! Salutations to the protector of the universe! Salutations! Salutations, to the source of the universe! Salutations! Salutations, to the embodiment of the universe! Salutations to You, Supreme Goddess!

In Hinduism, the spiritual practice (*sadhana*) of chanting the various holy names of the Divine is a central aspect of daily prayer and rituals. Many forms of God are honoured with a hymn of 108 names which describes their unique and divine qualities. Tulasi Devi can be also be worshipped by chanting Her eight sacred names and Her 108 names.

## The Eight Sacred Names of Tulasi Devi

*Vrindavani:* She who first manifested in the Vrindavana forest
*Vrinda:* She who is the Goddess of all plants and trees
*Visvapujita:* She who is worshipped by the whole universe
*Puspasara:* She who is the essence of all flowers
*Nandini:* She who gives faith and bliss to all
*Krishna-jivani:* She who is the very life and soul of Sri Krishna
*Visva-pavani:* She who purifies the whole world
*Tulasi:* She who has no comparison

## The 108 Names of Tulasi

Tulasī aṣṭottaraśata nāmāvaliḥ
1. Oṁ śrī tulasyai namaḥ
   Salutations to Sri Tulasi
2. Oṁ nandinyai namaḥ
   Salutations to Her who makes others happy
3. Oṁ devyai namaḥ
   Salutations to Her who is Devi, one who shines with divine powers
4. Oṁ śikhinyai namaḥ
   Salutations to Her whose flowers resemble the *shikha* (sacred tuft)

## *Tulasi Devi,* the Goddess of Devotion

5. Oṁ dhāriṇyai namaḥ
   Salutations to Her who is the Supporter of the universe
6. Oṁ dhātryai namaḥ
   Salutations to Her who is the Creator of the universe
7. Oṁ sāvitryai namaḥ
   Salutations to Her who is Savitri, the Goddess of the Sun
8. Oṁ satyasandhāyai namaḥ
   Salutations to Her who is truthful
9. Oṁ kālahāriṇyai namaḥ
   Salutations to Her who destroys Time
10. Oṁ gauryai namaḥ
    Salutations to Her who is in the form of Gauri (Shiva's wife)
11. Oṁ devagītāyai namaḥ
    Salutations to Her who is the song of the Gods
12. Oṁ davīyasyai namaḥ
    Salutations to Her who is most great
13. Oṁ padminyai namaḥ
    Salutations to Her who holds the lotus
14. Oṁ sitāyai namaḥ
    Salutations to Her who is in the form of Sita, beloved of Lord Rama
15. Oṁ rukmiṇyai namaḥ

*Traditional Worship and Rituals*

Salutations to Her who is in the form of Rukmini, wife of Sri Krishna

16. Oṁ priyabhuṣaṇāyai namaḥ
Salutations to Her who is pleased with ornaments

17. Oṁ śreyasyai namaḥ
Salutations to Her who is great

18. Oṁ śrīmatyai namaḥ
Salutations to Her who possesses *Sri*, auspiciousness

19. Oṁ mānyāyai namaḥ
Salutations to Her who is well-respected

20. Oṁ gauryai namaḥ
Salutations to Her who is of white colour

21. Oṁ gautamārcitāyai namaḥ
Salutations to Her who is worshipped by Sage Gautama

22. Oṁ tretāyai namaḥ
Salutations to Her who is in the form of the *Treta Yuga* (the age in which Sri Krishna lived)

23. Oṁ tripathagāyai namaḥ
Salutations to Her who travels through three paths

24. Oṁ tripādāyai namaḥ
Salutations to Her who has three legs

25. Oṁ traimūrtyai namaḥ

## *Tulasi Devi*, the Goddess of Devotion

Salutations to Her who is in the form of the *trimurti* (Brahma, Vishnu, and Shiva)

26. **Oṁ jagattrayāyai namaḥ**
Salutations to Her who is in the form of the three worlds (Bhur, Bhuvah, Suvah)

27. **Oṁ trāsinyai namaḥ**
Salutations to Her who is in the form of fear

28. **Oṁ gatrāyai namaḥ**
Salutations to Her who has a divine body

29. **Oṁ gatriyāyai namaḥ**
Salutations to Her who protects the body

30. **Oṁ garbhavāriṇyai namaḥ**
Salutations to Her who prevents rebirth in the womb (*samsara*)

31. **Oṁ śobhanāyai namaḥ**
Salutations to Her who is full of beauty

32. **Oṁ samāyai namaḥ**
Salutations to Her who is equananimous

33. **Oṁ dviradāyai namaḥ**
Salutations to Her who travels on an elephant

34. **Oṁ ārādyai namaḥ**
Salutations to Her who is worshipped

35. **Oṁ yajñavidyāyai namaḥ**
Salutations to Her who is the knowledge of sacrifice

36. **Oṁ mahāvidyāyai namaḥ**

## Traditional Worship and Rituals

Salutations to Her who is the great Knowledge

37. Oṁ guhyavidyāyai namaḥ
Salutations to Her who is the hidden Knowledge

38. Oṁ kāmākṣyai namaḥ
Salutations to Her who has beautiful, attractive eyes

39. Oṁ kulāyai namaḥ
Salutations to Her who is *Kula* (the spiritual tradition)

40. Oṁ śrīyai namaḥ
Salutations to Her who is *Sri*, auspiciousness

41. Oṁ bhūmyai namaḥ
Salutations to Her who is the Earth

42. Oṁ bhavitryai namaḥ
Salutations to Her who is in the form of Creation

43. Oṁ sāvitryai namaḥ
Salutations to Her who is in the form of the Gayatri mantra

44. Oṁ sarva-veda-vidām-varāyai namaḥ
Salutations to Her who is best among knowers of all the Vedas

45. Oṁ śamkhinyai namaḥ

Salutations to Her who holds the conch, and is the wife of Lord Vishnu (Shankin)

**46. Oṁ cakriṇyai namaḥ**
Salutations to Her who holds the discus, Her who is the wife of Vishnu (Cakrin), Her who is Lord Vishnu's Maya Shakti

**47. Oṁ cāriṇyai namaḥ**
Salutations to Her who possesses beauty

**48. Oṁ capalekṣaṇāyai namaḥ**
Salutations to Her who has beautiful, fluctuating eyes

**49. Oṁ pitāmbarāyai namaḥ**
Salutations to Her who wears yellow clothes

**50. Oṁ prīta-somāyai namaḥ**
Salutations to Her who is pleased with *Soma* (the juice of the Soma plant used in sacrifices)

**51. Oṁ saurasāyai namaḥ**
Salutations to Her who is beautiful *rasa*, who is supreme Bliss

**52. Oṁ akṣiṇyai namaḥ**
Salutations to Her who has beautiful eyes

**53. Oṁ ambāyai namaḥ**
Salutations to Her who is the Mother

**54. Oṁ sarasvatyai namaḥ**
Salutations to Her who is in the form of Sarasvati

## Traditional Worship and Rituals

55. Oṁ saṁśrayāyai namaḥ
    Salutations to Her who is the True Support
56. Oṁ sarva-devatyai namaḥ
    Salutations to Her who is in the form of all Deities
57. Oṁ visvāśrayāyai namaḥ
    Salutations to Her who is the Support of the universe
58. Oṁ sugandhinyai namaḥ
    Salutations to Her who has a pleasing fragrance
59. Oṁ suvāsanāyai namaḥ
    Salutations to Her who has pleasing clothes
60. Oṁ varadāyai namaḥ
    Salutations to Her who grants boons
61. Oṁ suśroṇyai namaḥ
    Salutations to Her who possesses beautiful thighs
62. Oṁ candra-bhāgāyai namaḥ
    Salutations to Her who wears the crescent moon
63. Oṁ yamunāpriyāyai namaḥ
    Salutations to Her to whom the Yamuna River is dear
64. Oṁ kāveryai namaḥ

Salutations to Her who is in the form of the Kaveri River

65. Oṁ maṇikarṇikāyai namaḥ
Salutations to Her who is in the form of the Manikarnika River

66. Oṁ arcinyai namaḥ
Salutations to Her who is in the form of worship

67. Oṁ sthāyinyai namaḥ
Salutations to Her who is unchanging

68. Oṁ dāna-pradāyai namaḥ
Salutations to Her who grants gifts

69. Oṁ dhanavatyai namaḥ
Salutations to Her who is the possessor of wealth

70. Oṁ śocya-mānasāyai namaḥ
Salutations to Her who cares about sorrowful people

71. Oṁ śucinyai namaḥ
Salutations to Her who is pure

72. Oṁ śreyasyai namaḥ
Salutations to Her who is great

73. Oṁ prīti-cintekṣaṇāyai namaḥ
Salutations to Her who wishes for others to have pleasing thoughts

74. Oṁ vibhūtyai namaḥ

Salutations to Her who is full of divine manifestations, who is full of divine glories
75. Oṁ ākṛtyai namaḥ
Salutations to Her who has a beautiful form
76. Oṁ āvirbhūtyai namaḥ
Salutations to Her who is manifested
77. Oṁ prabhāvinyai namaḥ
Salutations to Her who possesses great glory
78. Oṁ gandhinyai namaḥ
Salutations to Her who has a pleasing fragrance
79. Oṁ svarginyai namaḥ
Salutations to Her who is the possessor of *Svarga* (heaven)
80. Oṁ gadāyai namaḥ
Salutations to Her who is Gada, who holds a club, who is the wife of Lord Vishnu
81. Oṁ vedyāyai namaḥ
Salutations to Her who is fit to be known
82. Oṁ prabhāyai namaḥ
Salutations to Her who is effulgent Light
83. Oṁ sārasyai namaḥ
Salutations to Her who is in the form of the swan
84. Oṁ sarasi-vāsāyai namaḥ

Salutations to Her who dwells in water, who is the lotus

85. **Oṁ sarasvatyai namaḥ**
Salutations to Her who is in the form of Sarasvati, the Goddess of Wisdom

86. **Oṁ sāravatyai namaḥ**
Salutations to Her who is significant

87. **Oṁ rasinyai namaḥ**
Salutations to Her who possesses a sweet flavor

88. **Oṁ kālinyai namaḥ**
Salutations to Her who is in the form of Kali

89. **Oṁ śreyovatyai namaḥ**
Salutations to Her who possesses greatness

90. **Oṁ yāmāyai namaḥ**
Salutations to Her who is in the form of Time

91. **Oṁ brahma-priyāyai namaḥ**
Salutations to Her to whom Brahma, the Creator, is dear

92. **Oṁ śyāma-sundarāyai namaḥ**
Salutations to Her who is dark and beautiful

93. **Oṁ ratna-rūpinyai namaḥ**
Salutations to Her whose form is of jewels

94. **Oṁ śama-nidhinyai namaḥ**
Salutations to Her who is the treasure of control of the mind

## Seeds of Hope

95. Oṁ śatānandāyai namaḥ
    Salutations to Her who is Infinite Bliss
96. Oṁ śata-dyutāyai namaḥ
    Salutations to Her who is infinite brightness
97. Oṁ śiti-kaṇthāyai namaḥ
    Salutations to Her who has a cool throat
98. Oṁ prayāyai namaḥ
    Salutations to Her who surpasses all
99. Oṁ dhātryai namaḥ
    Salutations to Her who is the Protector
100. Oṁ śrī vrndāvanyai namaḥ
    Salutations to Sri Vrindavani, who dwells in Vrindavana
101. Oṁ kṛṣṇāyai namaḥ
    Salutations to Her who has a dark color
102. Oṁ bhakta-vatsalāyai namaḥ
    Salutations to Her who is dear to devotees
103. Oṁ gopikā-krīdāyai namaḥ
    Salutations to Her who sports with the Gopis
104. Oṁ harāyai namaḥ
    Salutations to Her who is in the form of Lord Shiva
105. Oṁ amṛta-rupiṇyai namaḥ
    Salutations to Her whose nature is Immortal
106. Oṁ bhūmyai namaḥ
    Salutations to Her who is the Earth

**107. Oṁ śrī kṛṣṇa-kāntāyai namaḥ**
Salutations to Her who is the beloved of Sri Krisna

**108. Oṁ śrī tulasyai namaḥ**
Salutations to Sri Tulasi

# Seeds of Hope

Tulasi is a gift given to us by the Divine Mother Herself. This blessed plant offers us many ways to rekindle our lost connection to the Divine within Nature. Tulasi Devi inspires us to express love and selflessness towards all beings in our thoughts, words and actions.

> *"Nature is a huge flower garden. The animals, birds, trees, plants and people are the garden's fully blossomed flowers of diverse colours. The beauty of this garden is complete only when all of these exist in unity, thereby spreading the vibrations of love and oneness. May all our minds become one in love. Let us work together to prevent these diverse flowers from withering away, so that the garden may remain eternally beautiful.*
>
> *"We must never lose our inner strength. Only weak minds see the dark side of everything and become confused. Those with optimism see the rays of God's grace in any kind of darkness. The lamp of this faith is within us. Light this lamp; it will shower light to guide each and every step we take. Let us not remain stuck in the painful memories of the wars and conflicts of days past. Forget the dark*

*history of hatred and rivalry and welcome a new era of faith, love and unity. For this, we must all work together. No effort, no matter how small, will ever be wasted. Even if just one flower blossoms in the middle of a desert, at least it is something. This is the attitude to develop when performing actions. Our abilities may be limited, but if we row the boat of life with the paddle of self-effort, then the wind of God's grace will definitely come to assist us.*

*"Life becomes fulfilled when humankind and Nature move together, hand in hand, in harmony. When melody and rhythm complement each other, the music becomes beautiful and pleasing to the ear. Likewise, when people live in accordance with the laws of Nature, life becomes like a beautiful song."*

*– Amma*

May we work together to spread Tulasi's seeds of hope around the world.

May the many treasures hidden within this sacred plant bless our lives.

# Hymn to Tulasi

*Namatulasi kalyani*
*Namo Vishnu priye shubhe*
*Namo moksha prade Devi*
*Namah sampad pradayini*

Salutations to Tulasi, the Auspicious,
Salutations to the beloved of Lord Vishnu,
Salutations to the Goddess who gives Liberation,
Salutations to the One who gives all prosperity.

# References

1. Kicel A, Kurowska A, Kalemba D. Composition of the essential oil of *Ocimum Sanctum* L. grown in Poland during vegetation. *Journal of Essential Oil Research* Mar/Apr 2005.

2. Singh S, Majumdar DK, Yadav MR. Chemical and pharmacological studies on fixed oil of *Ocimum Sanctum*. *Indian Journal of Experimental Biology* 1996;34(1):212-5.

3. Singh N, Hoette Y, Miller R. Tulasi – The Mother Medicine of Nature. 2002, Lucknow, India, International Institute of Herbal Medicine; ISBN 81-88007-00-5

4. Malviya, BK, Gupta PL. Growth promoting properties of *Ocimum sanctum* Linn. *Indian Journal of Pharmacology* 1971 33(6):126

5. Godhwani S, Godhwani JL, Vyas DS. *Ocimum sanctum*: an experimental study evaluating its anti-inflammatory, analgesic and antipyretic activity in animals. *Journal of Ethnopharmacol* November 1987;1(2):153-63.

6. Singh S, Majumdar DK. Evaluation of anti-inflammatory activity of fatty acids of *Ocimum sanctum* fixed oil. *Indian Journal of Experimental Biology* April 1997;35(4):380-3.

7. Singh S, Majumdar DK. Effect of fixed oil of *Ocimum sanctum* against experimentally induced arthritis and joint edema in laboratory animals. *Pharmaceutical Biology* July 1996;34(3):218-222(5).

8. Lasker S. Clinical trial of an indigenous preparation in osteoarthrosis of knee. *Medical Surgery* 1981;8:21.

9. Dixit, KS, Singh SP, Sinhar KN, Singh N, Kolhli RP. *Inula racemosa* (puskarmul) *Terminalia belerica* (bibhitaka)

*Ocimum sanctum* (tulsi) – a preliminary clinical trial in asthma patients. *Proc Int Sem Clin Pharmacol Dev Count KGMC Lucknow India* 1986; 2:22-27.

10. Sivarajin VV, Balachandran,I. Tulsi: Ayurvedic Drugs and Their Plant Sources. *Oxford FBH Publishing Co Pvt Ltd* 1994: 485-486.

11. Rajasekaran M, Sudhakaran C, Pradhan, SC, Bapna JS, Nair, AGR. Mast cell protective activity of ursolic acid – a triterpene from the leaves of *Ocimum sanctum* L. *J Drug Dev* 1989;l2(3):179-82.

12. Singh S, Agrawal S. Anti-asthmatic and anti-inflammatory activity of *Ocimum sanctum*. *Pharmaceutical Biology* 1991; 29(4):306-10.

13. Kumar P, et al. A clinical assessment of changes in cell-mediated immune response induced by gerifort. *The Antiseptic* 1982;10:560.

14. Singh N. A pharmaco-clinical evaluation of some ayurvedic crude plant drugs as anti-stress agents and their usefulness in some stress diseases of man. *Ann Nat Acad Ind Med* 1986;B(1):14-26.

15. Dixit K, Singh N. An assessment of immuno-modulator activity of some anti-stress Indian plants. *Proc Xth Int Cong Pharmacol* 1987;1:265.

16. Singh, SP, Sinha KN, Singh N, Kohli RP. *Inular racemosa* (pushkarmool), *Terminalia belerica* (bibhitaki) and *Ocimum sanctum* (tulsi) – a preliminary trial in asthma patients. *Proc Int Sem Clin Pharmacol Dev* 1986;1:18-21.

17. Rastogi RP, Mehrotra, BN. *Ocimum sanctum.* Compendium of Indian Medicinal Plants. *Publication and information directorate, CSIR, New Delhi* 1995b;4:510.

18. Kelm MA, Nair MG, Strasburg GM, DeWitt DL. Antioxidant and cyclooxygenase inhibitory phenolic compounds from *Ocimum sanctum* Linn. *Phytomedicine* March 2000;7(1):7-13.

19. Gupta S, Mediratta PK, Singh S, Sharma KK, Shukla R. Antidiabetic, antihypercholesterolaemic and antioxidant effect of *Ocimum sanctum (*Linn) Seed Oil. *Indian Journal Experimental Biology* April 2006;44(4):300-4

20. Singh SP, Singh N. Experimental Evaluation of Adaptogenic Properties of *Ocimum sanctum*. *Indian Journal of Pharmacology* 1978;10:74.

21. Bhargava KP, Singh, N. Anti-stress activity of *Ocimum sanctum* (Linn.*) Indian Journal of Medical Research* 1981; 73:443-451.

22. Singh N, Misra N. Experimental methods – tools for assessment of anti-stress activity in medicinal plants. *Journal of Bio Chemical Research* 1993;12(182):124-127.

23. Misra A, Misra PC, Singh N. Evaluation of ayurvedic herbal drugs on the damage caused by free radicals. *PhD Thesis, Dept of Pharmacology and Therapeutics, KGMC, Lucknow University* 1998.

24. Balanehru S, Nagarajan B. Protective effect of oleanolic acid and ursolic acid against lipid peroxidation. *Biochem Int* 1991;24(5):981-990.

25. Geetha R, Kedlaya DM, Vasudevan DM. Inhibition of Lipid Peroxidation by Botanical Extracts of *Ocimum sanctum*: in vivo and in vitro studies. *Life Sciences* November 2004;76(1): 19,21-28.

26. Arya DS, Nandave M, Ojha SK, Kumari S, Joshi S, Mohanty I. Myocardial salvaging effects of *Ocimum sanctum* in experimental model of myocardial necrosis: a haemo-

dynamic, biochemical and histoarchitectiral assessment. *Current Science* September 2006;91(5).

27. Sood S, Narang D, Thomas MK, Gupta YK, Maulik SK. Effect of *Ocimum sanctum* Linn. on cardiac changes in rats subjected to chronic restraint stress. *Journal of Ethnopharmacol* Dec 2006;108(3):423-7.

28. Ganasoundari A, Devi PU. Protection against radiation-induced chromosome damage in mouse bone marrow by *Ocimum sanctum*. Mutation Research/Fundamental and *Molecular Mechanisms of Mutagenesis* February 1997;373(2)271-276.29. Ganasoundari A, Devi PU, Rao AR. Enhancement of Bone Marrow Radioprotection and Reduction of WR-2721 Toxicity by *Ocimum sanctum*. *Mutation Research* February 1998;397(2):303-12.

30. Karthikeyan K, Ravichandran P, Govindasamy S. Chemopreventive effect of *Ocimum sanctum* on DMBA-induced hamster buccal pouch carcinogenesis. *Oral Oncology* January 1999; 35(1):112-119.

31. Banerjee S, Prashar R, Kumar A, Rao AR. Modulatory influence of alcoholic extract of *Ocimum* leaves on carcinogen-metabolizing enzyme activities and reduced glutathione levels in mouse. *Nutr-Cancer* 1996;25(2):205-17.

32. Rastogi S, Shukla Y, Paul BN, Chowdhuri DK, Khanna SK, Das M. Protective effect of *Ocimum sanctum* on 3-methylcholanthrene,7, 12 dimethyl benz(a) anthracene and alfatoxin B-1 induced skin tumorigenesis in mice. *Toxicology and Applied Pharmacology* November 2007;224(3,1):228-240.

33. Sharma P, Kulshreshtha S, Sharma AL. Anti-cataract activity of *Ocimum sanctum* on experimental cataract. *Indian Journal of Pharmacology* 1998;30(1):16-20.

34. Gupta, SK, Srivastava S, Trivedi D, Joshi S, Halder N. *Ocimum sanctum* modulates selenite-induced catarctogenic changes and prevents rat lens opacification. *Current Eye Research* July 2005;30(7):583-91.

35. Singh S, Malhortra M, Majumdar DK. Antibacterial activity of *Ocimum sanctum* L. fixed oil. *Indian J Exp Biol* September 2005;43(9):835-7.

36. Patel VK, Bhatt HVK. Folklore therapeutic indigenous plants in periodontal disorders in India. *Int J Clin pharmacol Ther Toxicol* 1988;26(4):176-184.

37. Shokeen P, Ray K, Bala M, Tandon V. Preliminary studies on activity of *Ocimum sanctum*, *Drynaria quercifolia*, and *Annona squamosa* against neisseria gonorrhoeae. *Sex Transm Dis* February 2005;32(2):106-11.

38. Geetha R, Vasudevan DM, Kedlaya R, Deepa S, Ballal M. Activity of *Ocimum sanctum* (the traditional Indian medicinal plant) against the enteric pathogens. *Indian J Med Sci* August 2001;55(8):434-8,472.

39. Gupta, G, Charan S. Antimicrobial and Immuno-modulating effects of *Ocimum sanctum* (shyama tulsi) against infectious bursal disease virus infection in chickens as model. *Indian Journal of Comparative Microbiology, Immunology and Infectious Diseases* 2005;26(2).

40. Rajalakshmi G, et al. Role of Tulsi (*Ocimum sanctum*) in viral hepatitis. *J Res Ayur Sid* 1988;9:118.

41. Das, SK, et al. *Ocimum sanctum* (tulsi) in the treatment of viral encephalitis. *The Antiseptic* 1983:1-5.

42. Yamasaki K, et al. Anti-HIV-1 activity of herbs in labiatae. *Biol Pharm Bull* 1998;21(8):829-833.

43. Asha MK, Prahantah D, Murali B, Padmaja R, Amit A. Anthelmintic activity of essential oil of *Ocimum sanctum* and eugenol. *Filtoterapia* August 2001;72(6):669-70.

44. Banu, NJ, et al. S. Mitochondrial malate dehydrogenase and malic enzyme of a filaria worm *setari digitaria*: Some Properties and Effects of Drugs and Herbal Extracts. *Jpn. J. Med. Sci. Biol* 1992;45(3):137-150.

45. Roy, RG, et al. Study on inhalation therapy by an indigenous compound *P. vivax* and *P. falciparum* infections. *Indian Journal Medical Research* 1976;64(10):1451-1455.

46. Gill K, Malik OP, Kalidhar SB, Mishra RC, Malik MS. Honey bee repellent activity of leaf extract and essential oil of *Ocimum sanctum* and isolation of a new compound. *Department of Chemisty and Physics, CCS Haryana Agricultural University, Hisar-125004, India.*

47. Rai V, Iyer U, Mani UV. Effect of tulasi (*Ocimum sanctum*) leaf powder supplementation on blood sugar levels, serum lipids and tissue lipids in diabetic rats. *Plant Foods for Human Nutrition* 1997;50(1):9-16(8).

48. Chattopadhyay RR. A comparative evaluation of some blood sugar lowering agents of plant origin. *Journal of Ethnopharmacology* November 1999;67(3):367-372.

49. Grover JK, Yadav S, Vats V. Medicinal plants of India with anti-diabetic potential. *Journal of Ethnopharmacology* June 2002;81(1):81-100.

50. Rai V, Ficn UV, Mani UM. Effect of *Ocimum sanctum* leaf powder on blood lipoproteins, glycated proteins and total amino acids in patients with non-insulin-dependent diabetes mellitus. *Journal of Nutritional & Environmental Medicine* June 1997;7(2):113-118(6).

51. Hannan, JMA, Marenah, L., Ali, L., Rokeya, B., Flatt, P.R., Adbel-Waheb, YHA. *Ocimum sanctum* Leaf Extracts Stimulate Insulin Secretion from Perfused Pancreas, Isolated Islets and Clonal Pancreatic ß-cells. *Journal of Endocrinology*, 2006; 189:127-136

52. Agrawal, P., Rai, V., Singh, RB. Randomized Placebo-Controlled, Single Blind Trial of Holy Basil Leaves in Patients with Non-insulin-Dependent Diabetes Mellitus. Int J *Clin Pharmacol Ther*, September 1996;34(9):406-9

53. Hannan, JMA, Marenah, L., Ali, L., Rokeya, B., Flatt, P.R., Adbel-Waheb, YHA. *Ocimum sanctum* Leaf Extracts Stimulate Insulin Secretion from Perfused Pancreas, Isolated Islets and Clonal Pancreatic ß-cells. *Journal of Endocrinology*, 2006;189:127-136

54. Mitra A. Composite of Tulsi leaves, Amla, bitter gourd, gurmur leaves, jamun fruit and seed in type 2 diabetic patients. *Journal of Clinical and Diagnostic Research* December 2007;6:511-520.

55. Singh S, Majumdar DK. Evaluatoin of the gastric anti-ulcer activity of fixed oil of *Ocimum sanctum* (Holy Basil). *Journal of Ethnopharmacology* April 1999;65(1):13-19.

56. Dharmani P, Kuchibhotla VK, Maurya R, Srivastava S, Gautam Palit G. Evaluation of anti-ulcerogenic and ulcer-healing properties of *Ocimum sanctum* Linn. *Journal of Ethnopharmacology* August 2004;93(2-3):197-2006.

57. Singh S, Majumbar DK. Evaluation of gastric ulceractivity of fixed oil of *Ocimum sanctum*. *Journal of Ethnopharmacology* 1999;65:13-19.7.

58. Jalil A., et al. Clinical trial of *Ocimum sanctum* in peptic ulcer and hyperacidity patients. *J Res Ind Med* 1970;4(2):238-239.

## References

59. Prakash P, Gupta N. Therapeutic uses of *Ocimum sanctum* Linn (tulsi) with a note of eugenol and its pharmacological actions: a short review. *Indian Journal of Physiol Pharmacology* 2005;49(2):125-131.

60. Khanna N, Bhatia J. Antinociceptive action of *Ocimum sanctum* (tulsi) in mice: possible mechanisms involved. *Journal of Ethnopharmacology* October 2003;88(2-3):293-29.

61. Bhargava KP, Singh N. Anti-stress activity of *Ocimum sanctum* Linn. *Indian Journal of Medical Research* 1981;73:443-451.

62. Sethi J, Singh S, Sood S, Talwar A, Seth S. Antistressor activity of *Ocimum sanctum* (tulsi) against experimentally induced oxidative stress in rabbits. *Methods Find Exp Clin Pharmacol* 2007;29(6):411.

63. Maity TK, Mandal SC, BP Saha, Pal M. Effect of *Ocimum Sanctum* roots extract on swimming performance in mice. *Phytotherapy Research* 14(2):120-121.

64. Archana R, Namasivayam AA. Comparative study of different crude extracts of *Ocimum sanctum* on noise stress. *Phytotherapy Research* September 2002;16(6):579-80.

65. Sembulingam K, Sembulingam P, Namasivayam A. Effect of *Ocimum Sanctum* Linn on the changes of central cholinergic system inducted by acute noise stress. *Journal of Ethnopharmacol* January 2005;96(3):477-82.

66. Ishida M, Okubo T, Koshimizu K, Daito H, Tokuda H, Kin T, Yamamoto T, and Yamazaki N. Topical preparations containing ursolic acid and/or oleanoic acid for prevention of skin cancer. *Chemical Abstract* 1990;113,12173y.

67. Joshi H, Parle M. Evaluation of nootropic potential of *Ocimum Sanctum* Linn. in Mice. *Indian J Exp Biol* February 2006;44(2):133-6.

68. Prakash J, Gupta SK. Chemopreventative activity of *Ocimum Sanctum* seed oil. *Journal of Ethnopharmacolgy* September 2001;72(1-2):29-34.

69. Karthikeyan K, Gunasekaran P, Ramamurthy, Govindasamy S. Anticancer activity of *Ocimum sanctum*. *Parmaceutical Biology* October 1999;37(4):285-290(6).

70. Karthikeyan K, Ravichandran, P, Govindasamy S. Chemopreventive effect of *Ocimum sanctum* on DMBA-induced hamster buccal pouch carcinogenesus. *Oral Oncology* July 1999;35(1):112-119.

71. Liu J. Pharmacology of oleanolic acid and ursolic acid. *Journal of Ethnopharmacology* December 1995;49(2):57-68.

72. Devi UP, Nayak V, Kamath R. Lack of solid tumour protection by *Ocimum* extract and its flavonoids orientin and vicenin. *Current Science* May 2004; 86(10):1401-1404.

73. Bhartiya US, Raut YS, Joseph IJ. Protective effect of *Ocimum sanctum* L. after high-dose 131iodine exposure in mice: an in vivo study. *Laboratory Nuclear Medicine Section, Radiochemistry & Isotope Group PMID*: 16924835.

74. Devi PU., Bisht KS, Vinitha M. A comparative study of radioprotection by *Ocimum* flavonoids and synthetic aminothiol protectors in the mouse. *Br J Radiol* July 1998;71(847):782-4.

75. Mediratta PK, Sharma KK, Singh S. Evaluation of immuno-modulatory potential of *Ocimum Sanctum* seed oil and its possible mechanism of action. *Journal of Ethnopharmacology* April 2002;80(1):15-20.

76. Logambal SM, Venkatalakshmi S, Dinakaran MR. Immunostimulatory effect of leaf extract of *Ocimum sanctum* Linn. in oreochromis mossambicus (Peters). *Journal Hydrobiolgia* July 2000;430:1-3.

# References

77. Rastogi S, Shukla Y, Paul BN, Chowdhuri DK, Khanna SK, Das M. Protective effect of *Ocimum sanctum* on 3-methycholanthrene, 7, 12-dimethylbenz(a)anthracen. *Toxical Appl Parmacol* 2007:0

78. Singh S, Rehan HM, Majumdar DK. Effect of *Ocimum sanctum* fixed oil on blood pressure, bloodclotting time and pentobarbitone-induced sleeping time. *J Ethenopharmacol* December 2001;18(2-3):138-43.

79. Halim EM, Mukhopadhyay AK. Effect of *Ocimum Sanctum* (tulsi) and vitamin E on biochemical parameters and retinopathy in streptozotocin induced diabetic rats. *Indian Journal of Clinical Biochemistry* 2006;21(2):181-188.

80. Balanehru S, Nagarajan B. Protective effect of oleanolic acid and ursolic acid against lipid peroxidation. *Biochem Int* July 1999;24(5):981-90

81. Sunanda P, Kar A. *Ocimum sanctum* leaf extract in the regulation of thyroid function in the male mouse. *Pharmacologica Research* August 1998;38(2):107-110.

82. Rajeshwari S. *Ocimum sanctum*, The Indian home remedy. *Current Medical Science* March-April 1992.

83. Batta SK, Santhakumari G. The antifertility effect of *Ocimum sanctum* and *Hibiscus Rosa Sinensis*. *Indian Journal of Medical Research* 1971;59:777-781.

84. Nagarajun S, Jain HC, Aulakh GS. Indigenous Plants Used in Fertility Control. Cultivation and Utilization of Medicinal Plants. Editors: Atal, C.K. and Kapoor, B.M.*(Published by PID CSIR)* 1989: 558.

85. Reghunandana R, Sood S, Reghunandana V, Mehta RM, Singh GP. Effect of *Ocimum sanctum* Linn (tulsi) extract on testicular function. *Indian Journal of Medical Research* 1995;49(4):83-87.

86. Ahmed M, Ahamed RN, Aladakatti RH, Ghosesawar MG. Reversible anti-fertility effect of benzene extract of *Ocimum sanctum* leaves on sperm parameters and fructose content in rats. *J Basic Clin Physiol Pharmacol* 2002;13(1):51-9.

87. Multilingual Multiscript Plant Name Database- Sorting Ocimum Names. 2008 [online]. The University of Melbourne. Available from

http://www.plantnames.unimelb.edu.au/Sorting/Ocimum.html

88. Oudhia, P. 2003 [online]. Major Ocimum species (Tulsi) of Chhattisgarh, India : Natural Occurrence, Traditional Medicinal Knowledge and Trade, Research Note

Available from http://www.botanical.com/site/column_poudhia/80_tulsi.html

[Accessed 9 August 2008].

89. Spice Pages. 2008. *Basil* [online]. Available from URL http://www.uni-graz.at/~katzer/engl/Ocim_bas.html#part [Accessed 5 August 2008].

90. Vanamali. Sri Devi Lila, The Play of the Divine Mother. *Aryan Books International* 2006, ISBN 817305304-9

CPSIA information can be obtained
at www.ICGtesting.com
Printed in the USA
BVHW070037050720
582971BV00006B/911